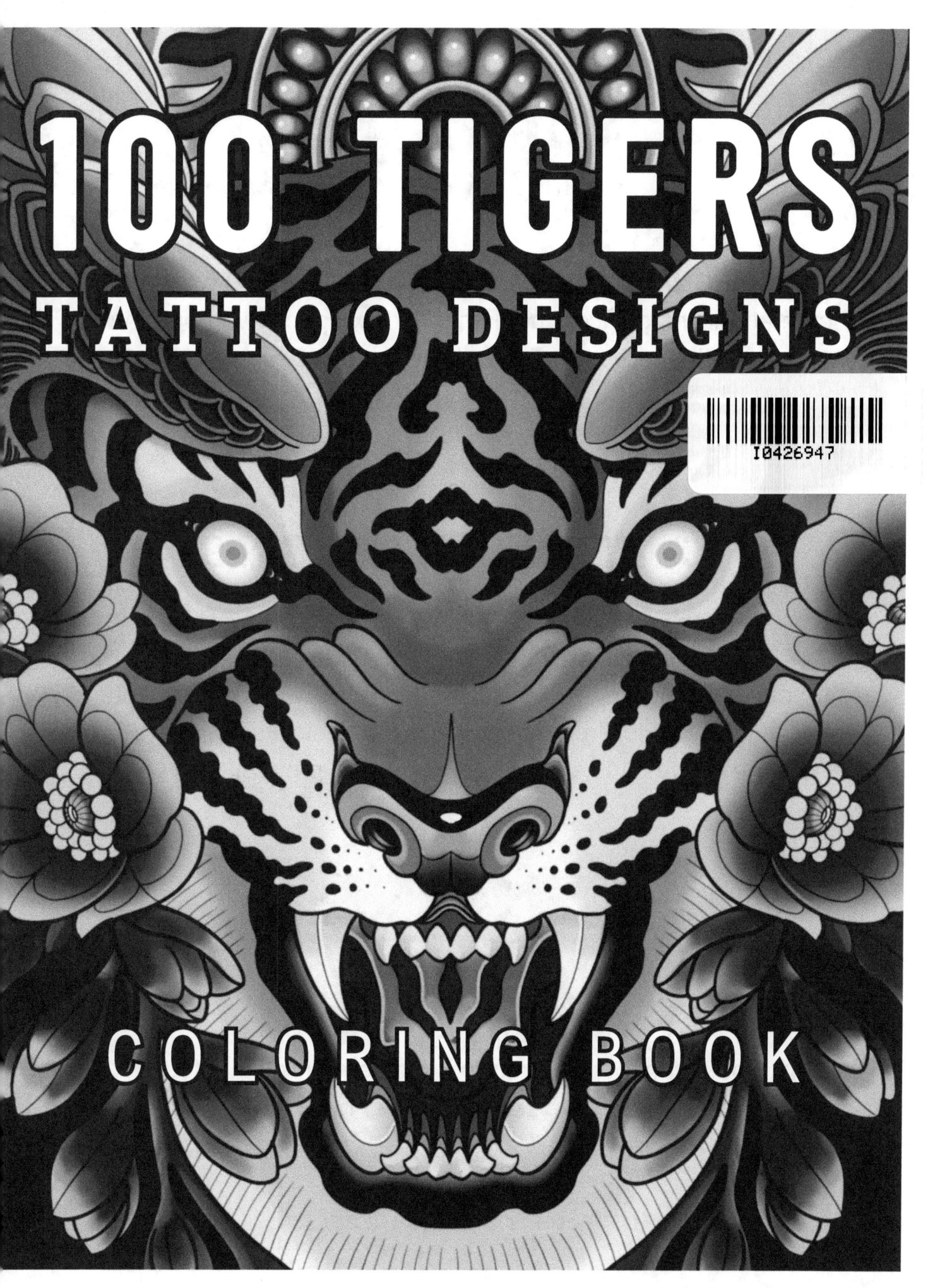

100 TIGERS
TATTOO DESIGNS
COLORING BOOK

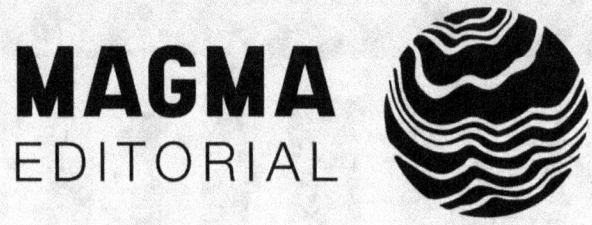

MAGMA
EDITORIAL

From **MAGMA EDITORIAL** by @JAISIELTATTOO we have created this magnificent book inspired by tigers. We hope that you enjoy this unique therapeutic coloring experience.

100 TIGERS
TATTOO DESIGNS
COLORING BOOK

If you liked and enjoyed our hard work, we would appreciate to know your opinion regarding our book. Help us by rating it on Amazon so we can keep bringing you new products.

This book cannot be scanned, copied or distributed in any establishment without the permission of MAGMA EDITORIAL.

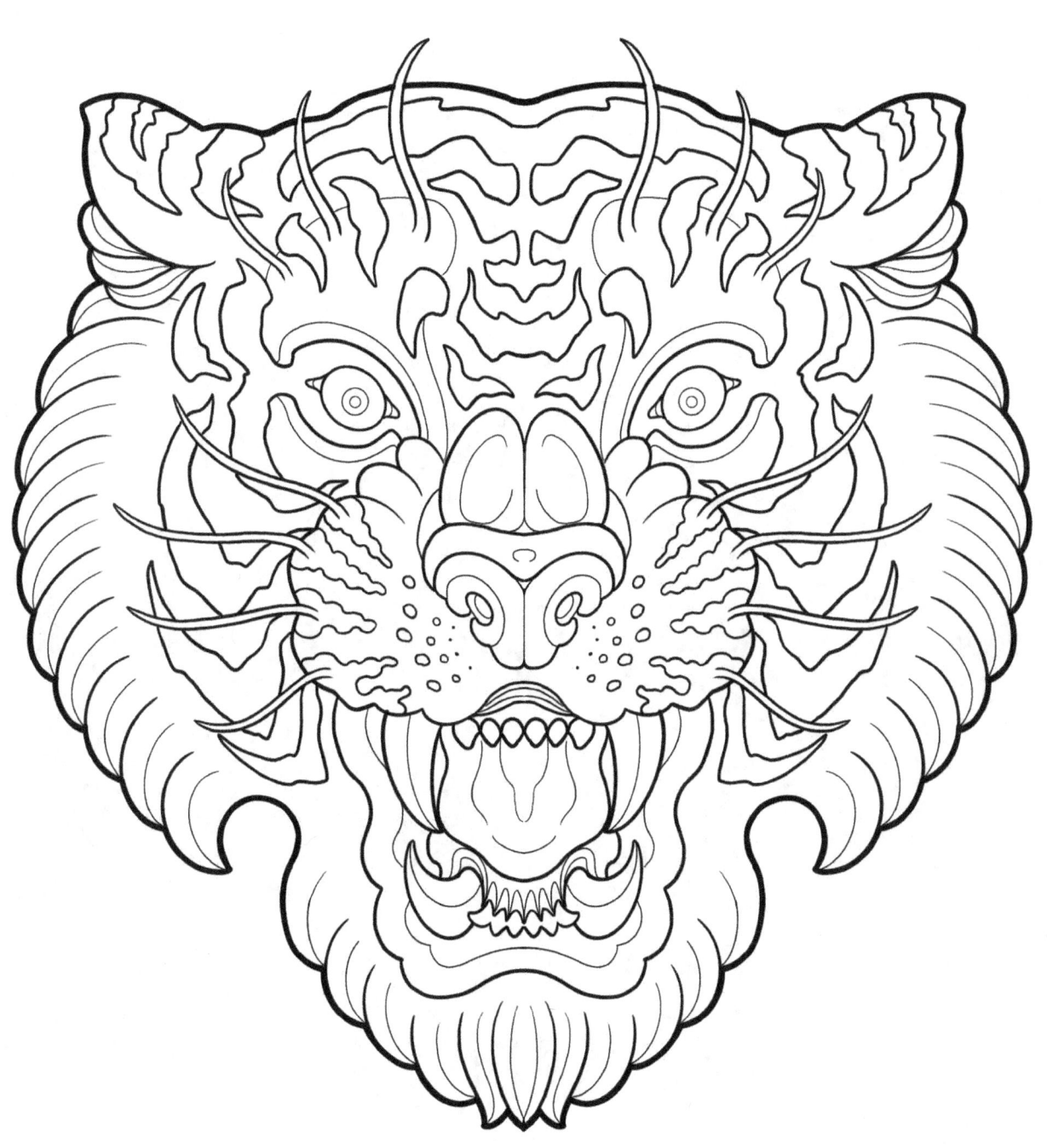

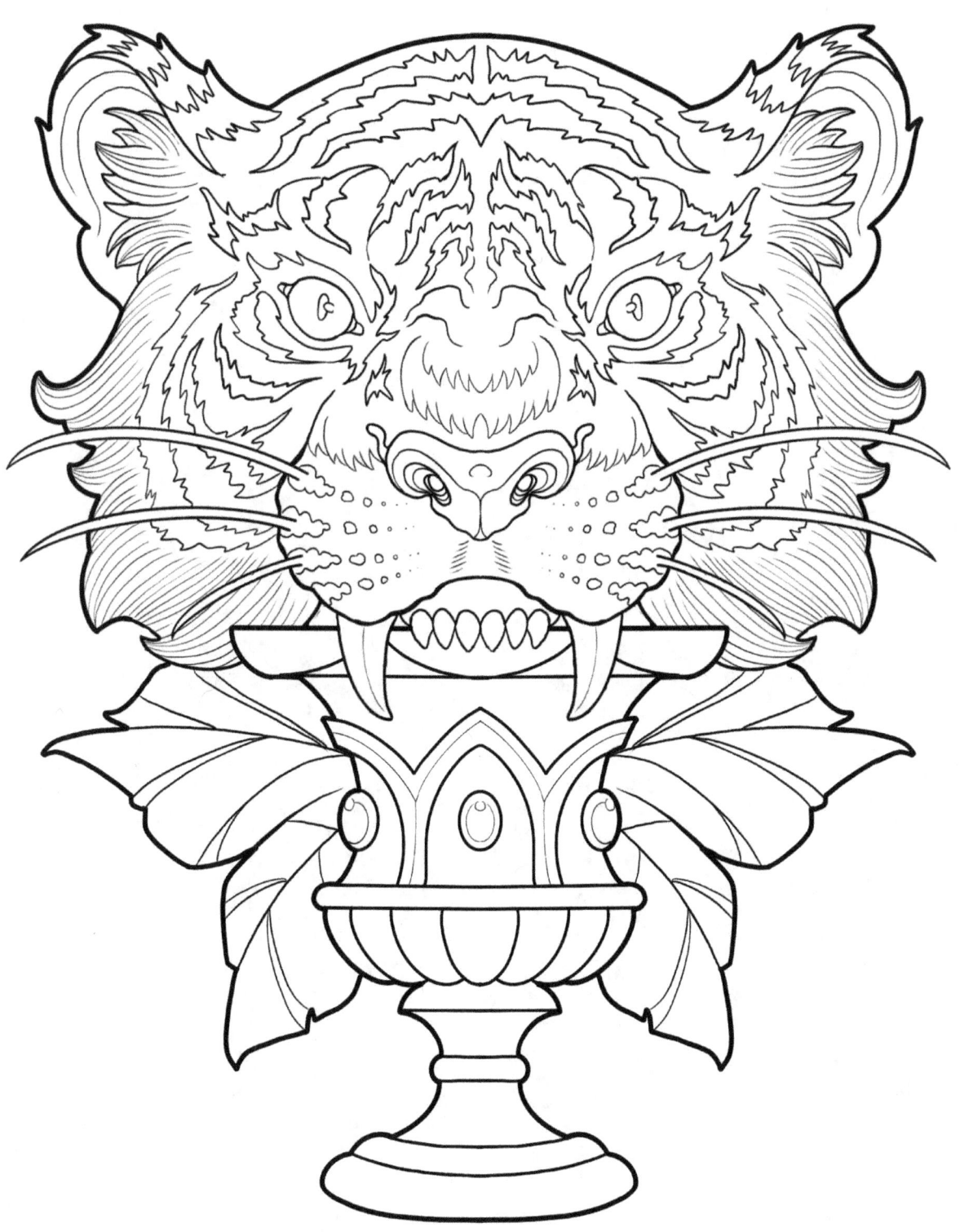

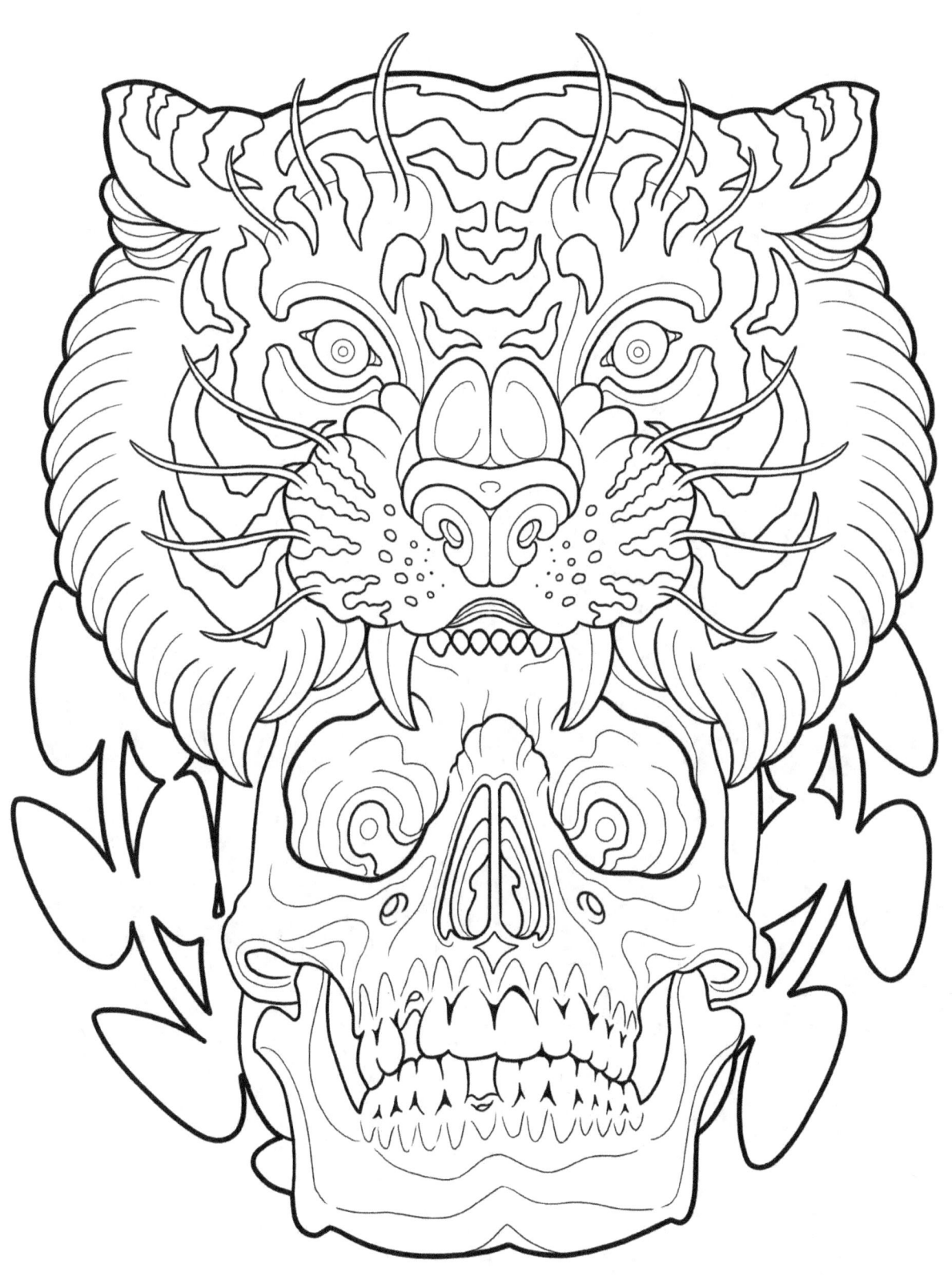

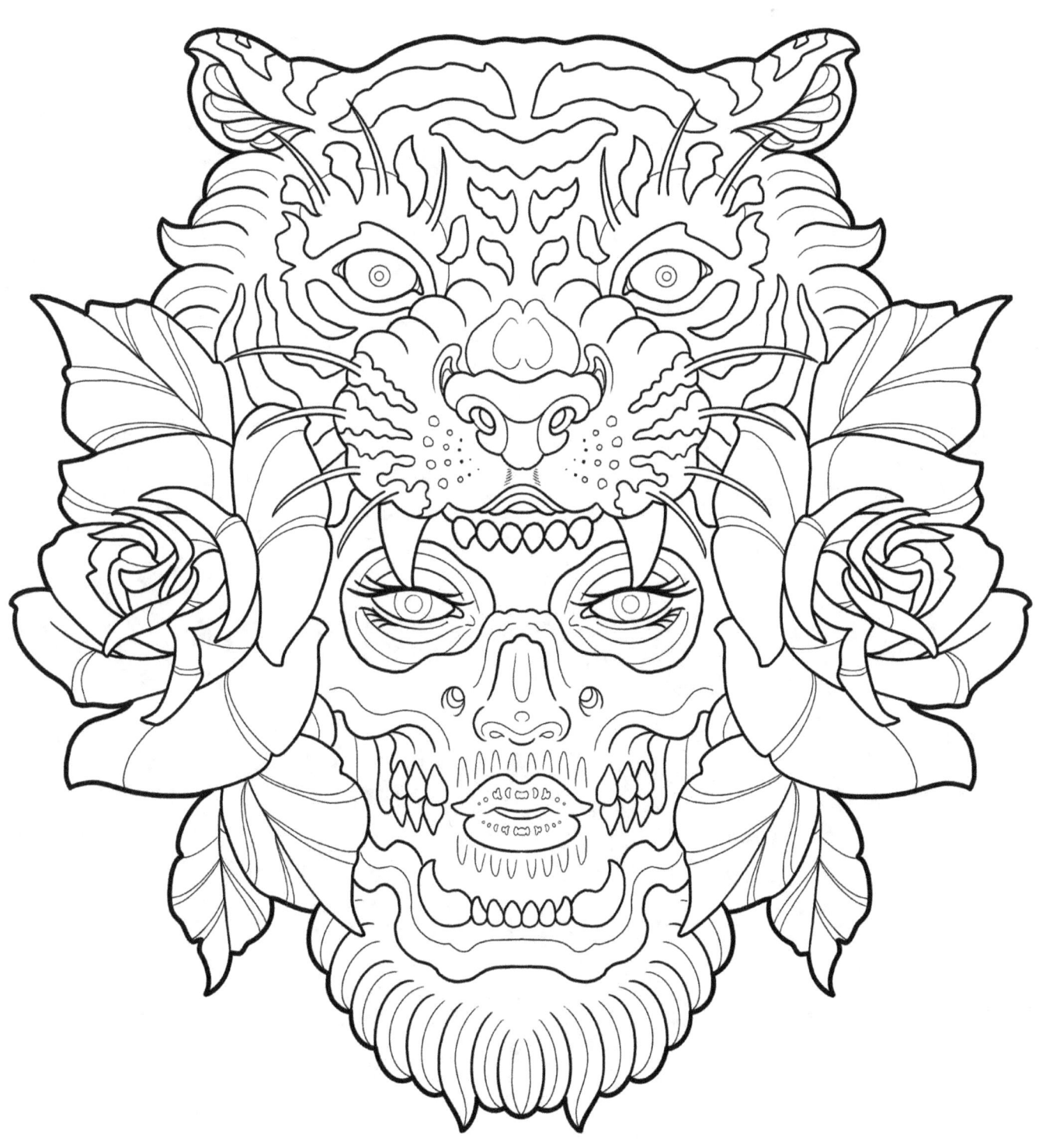

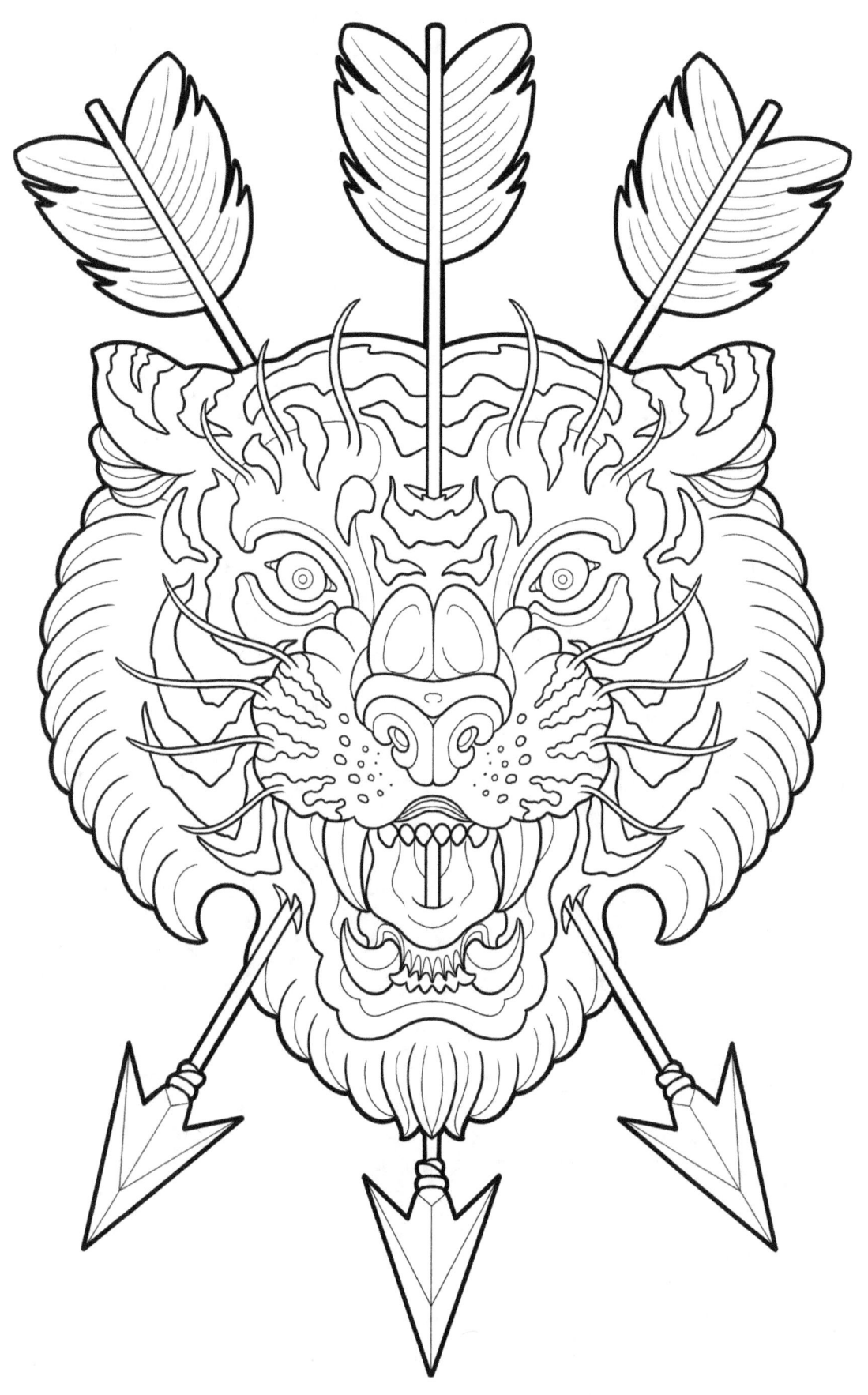

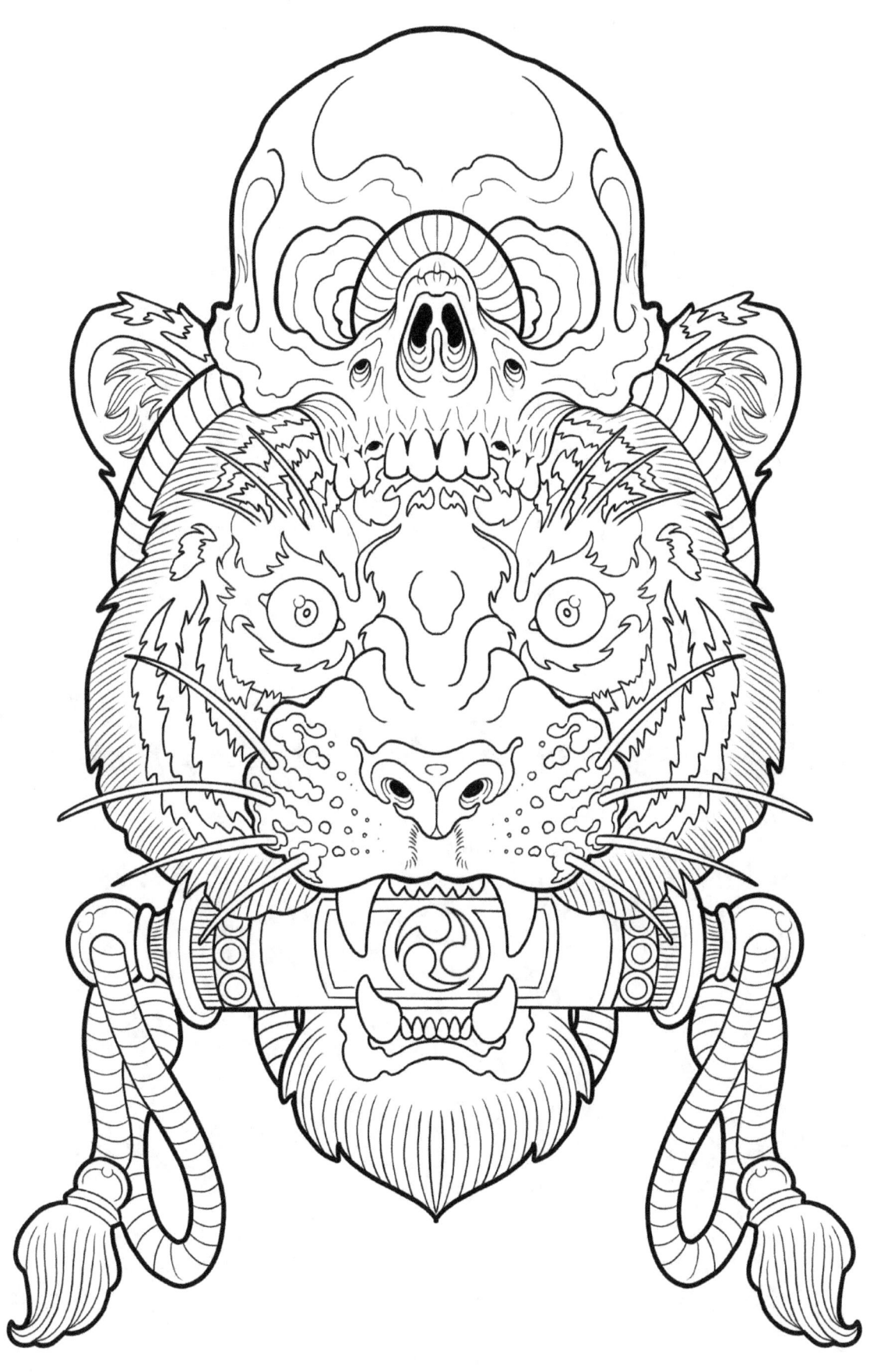

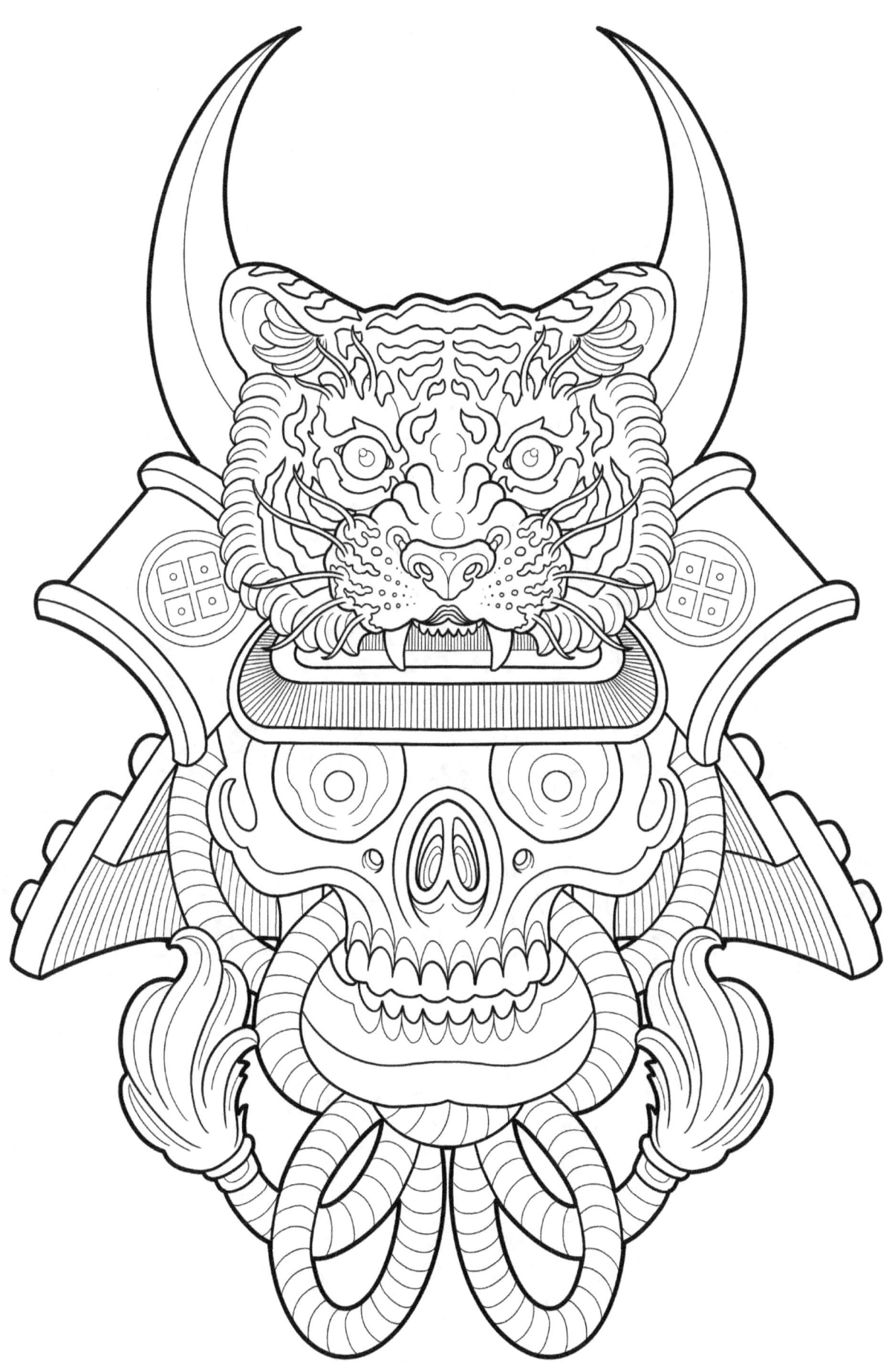

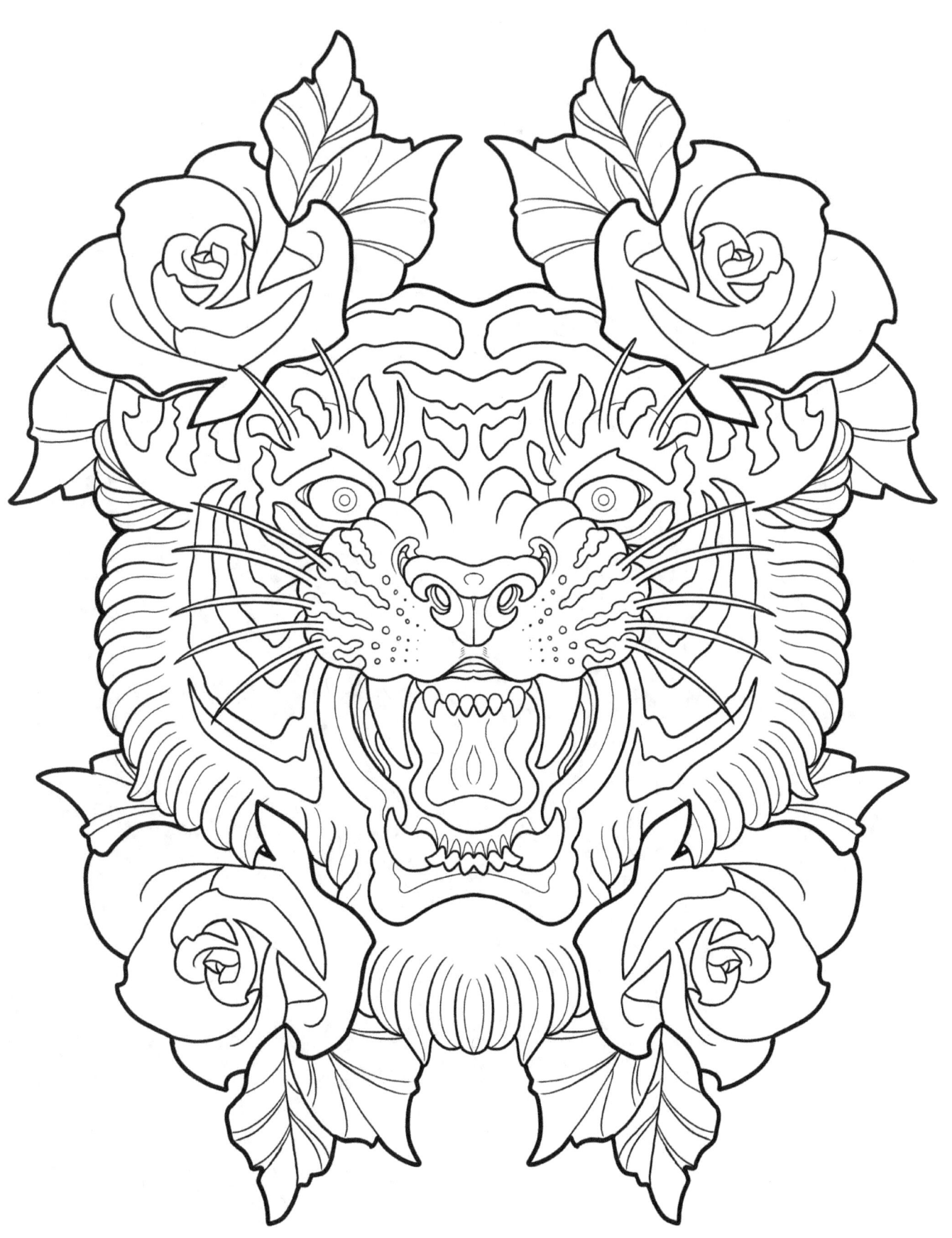

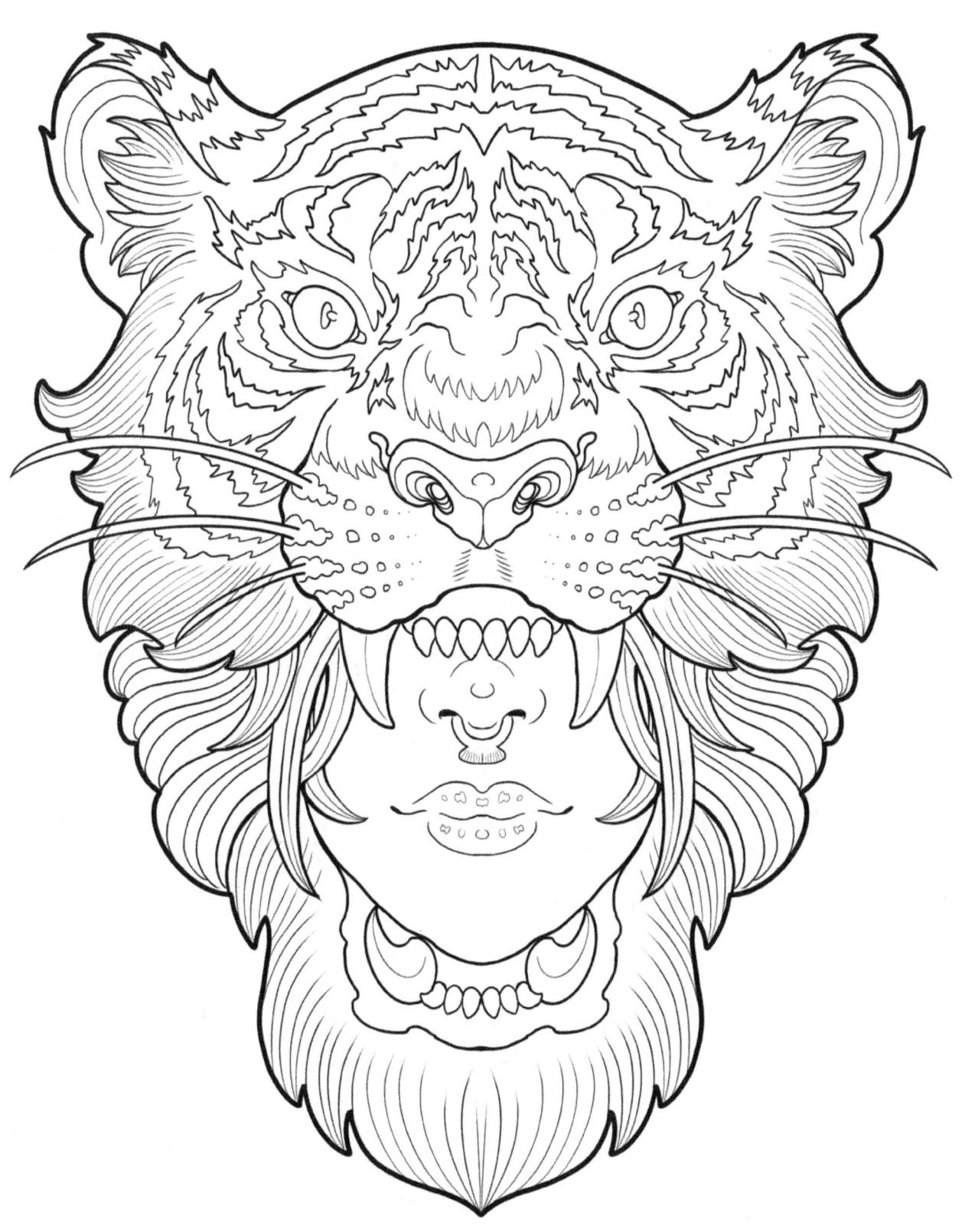

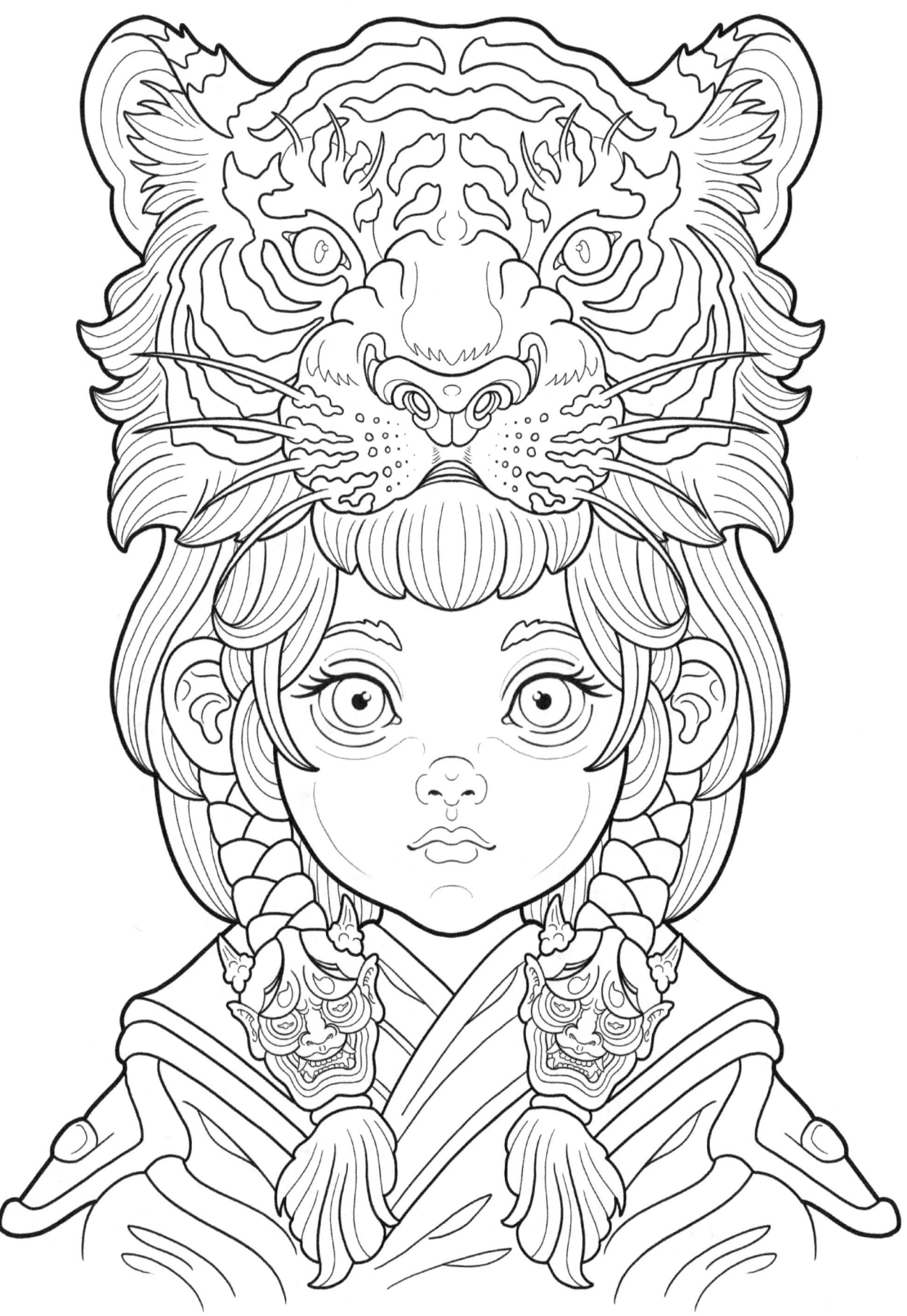

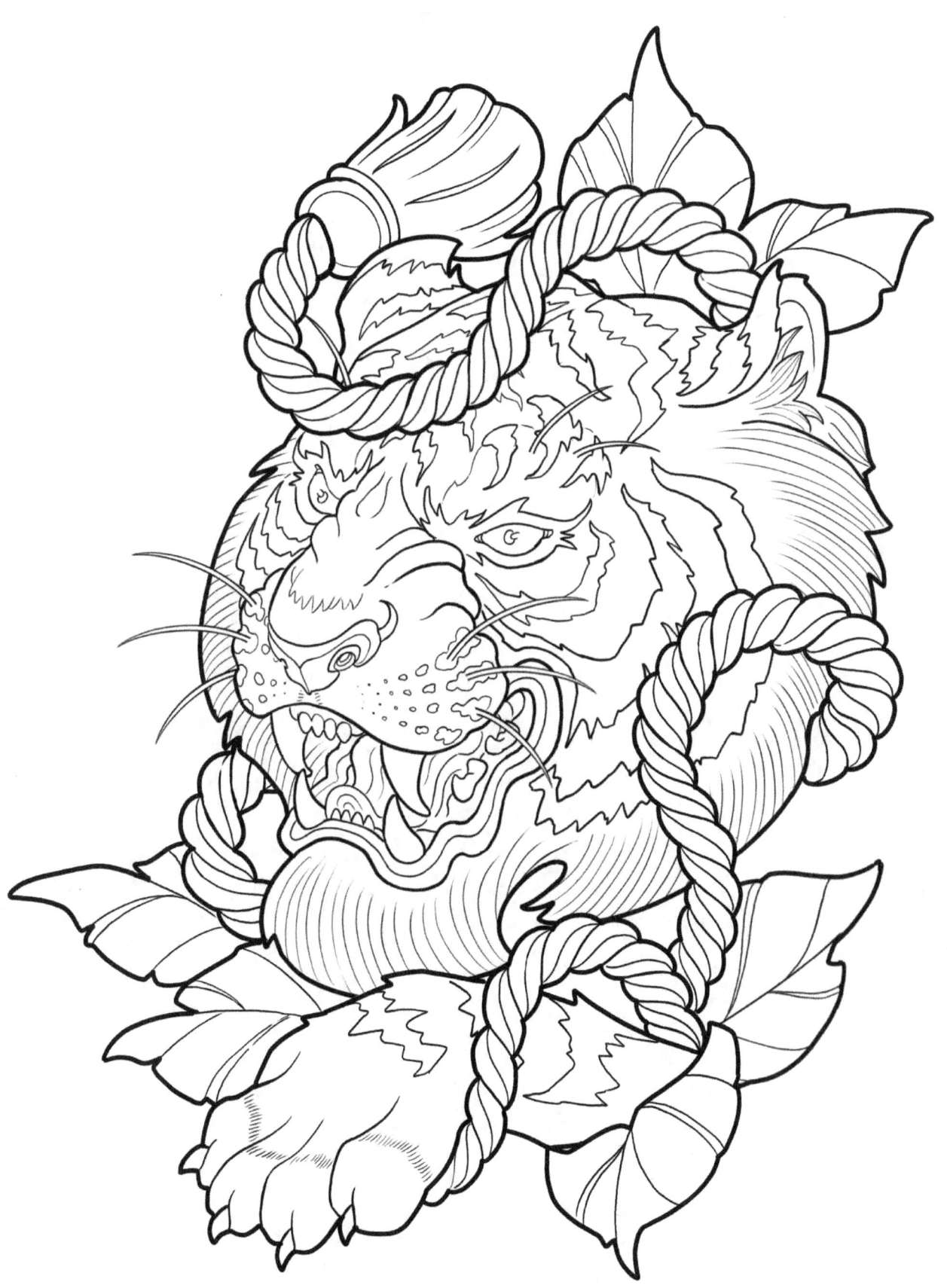

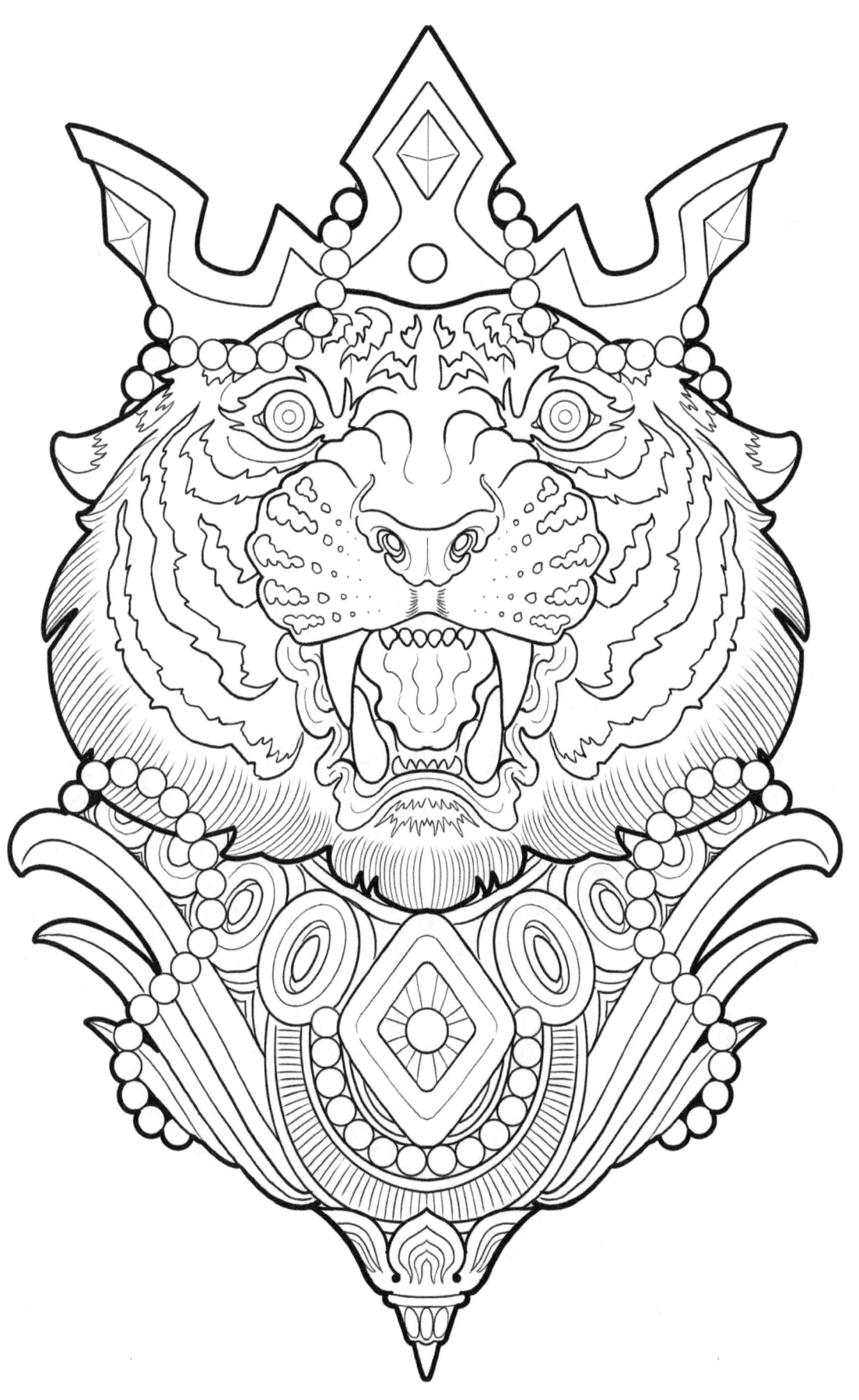

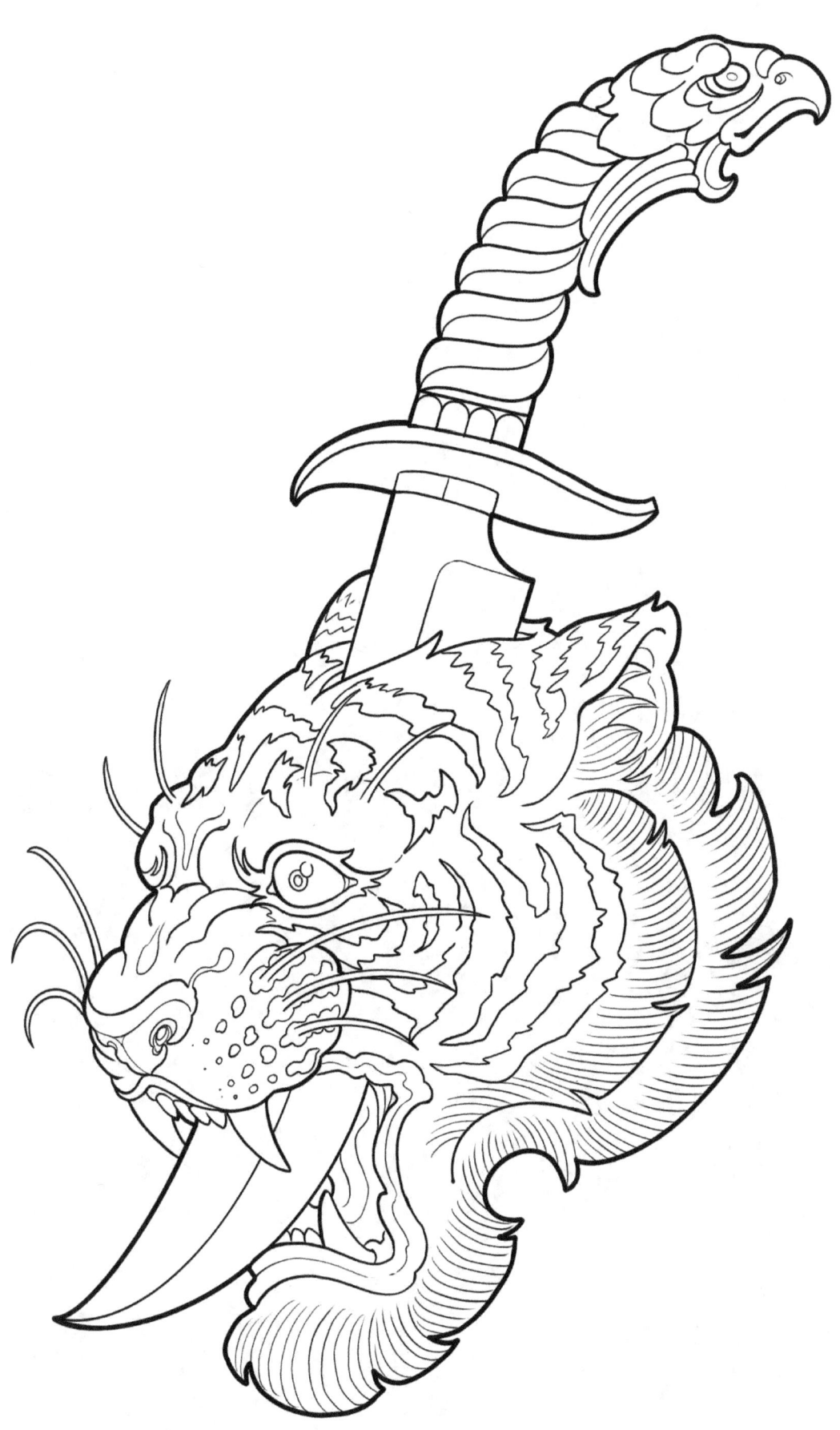

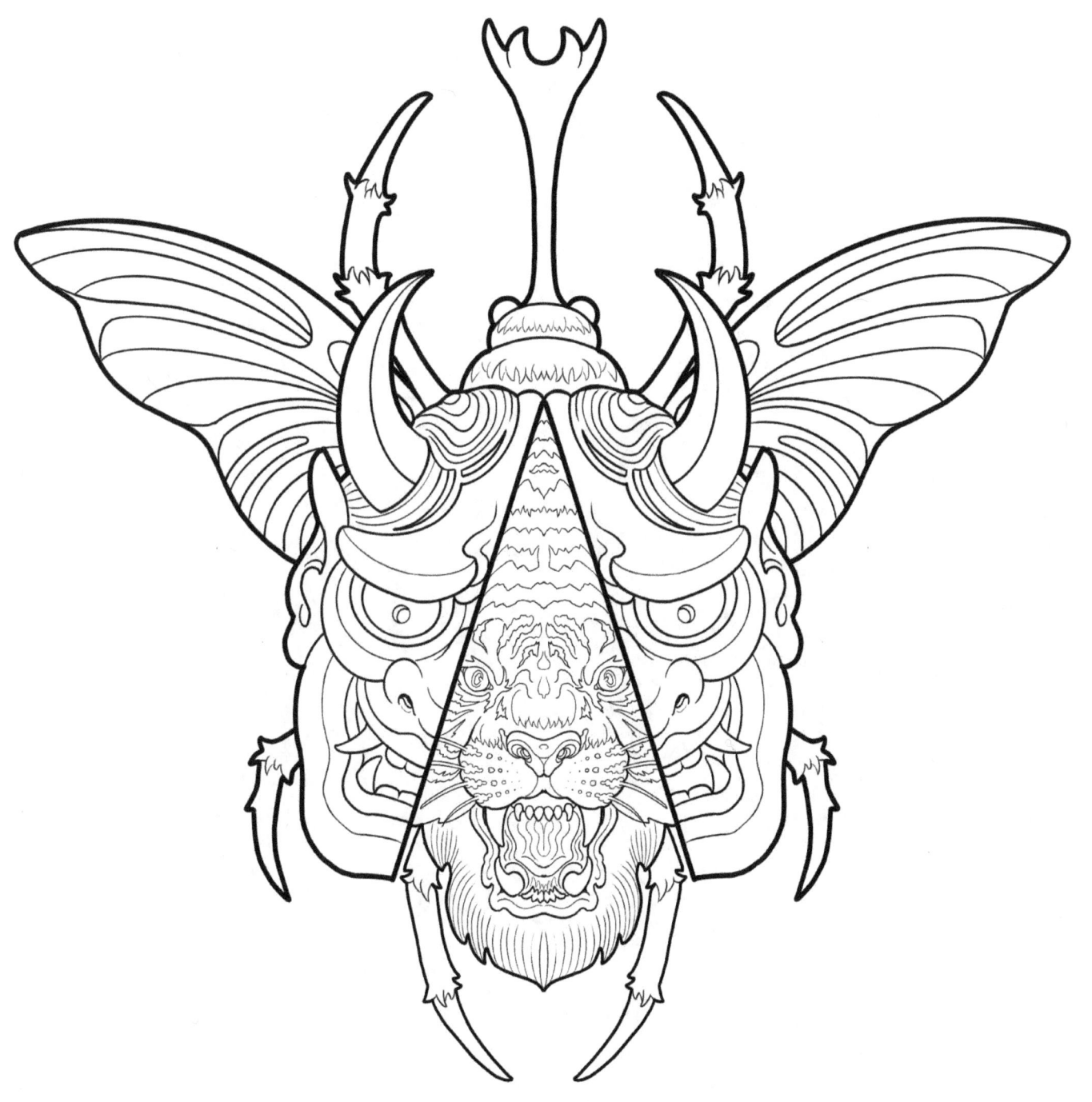

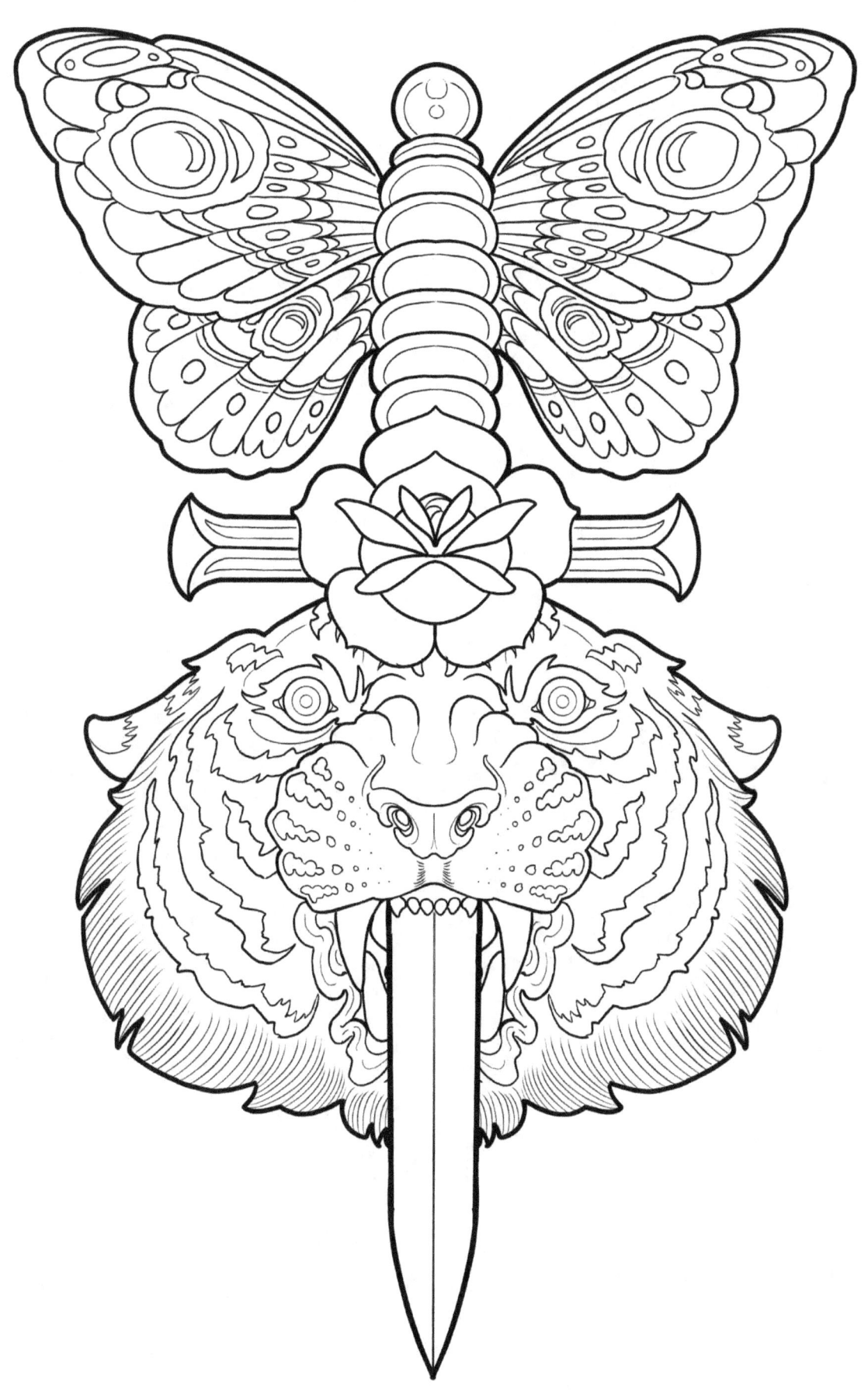

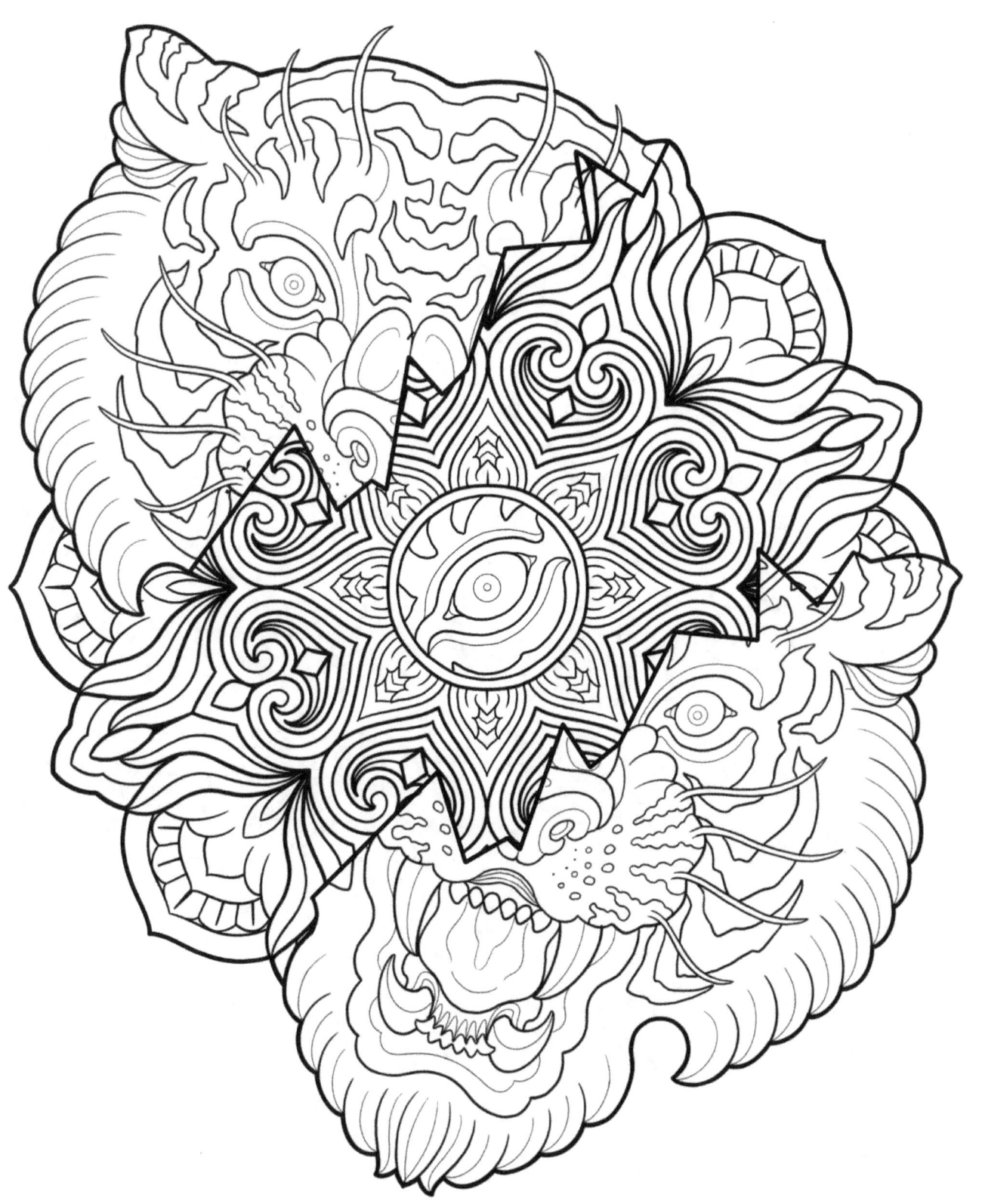

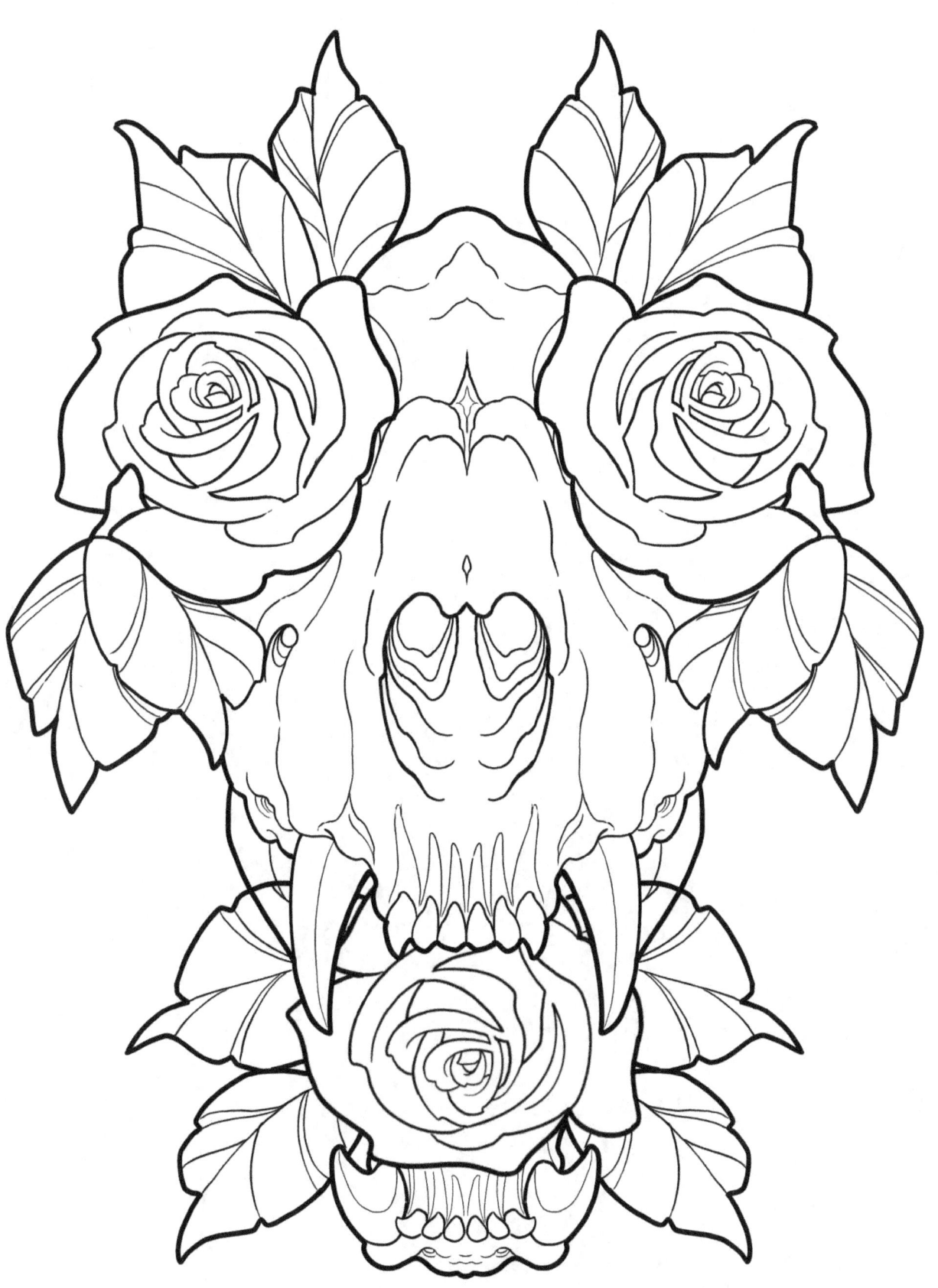

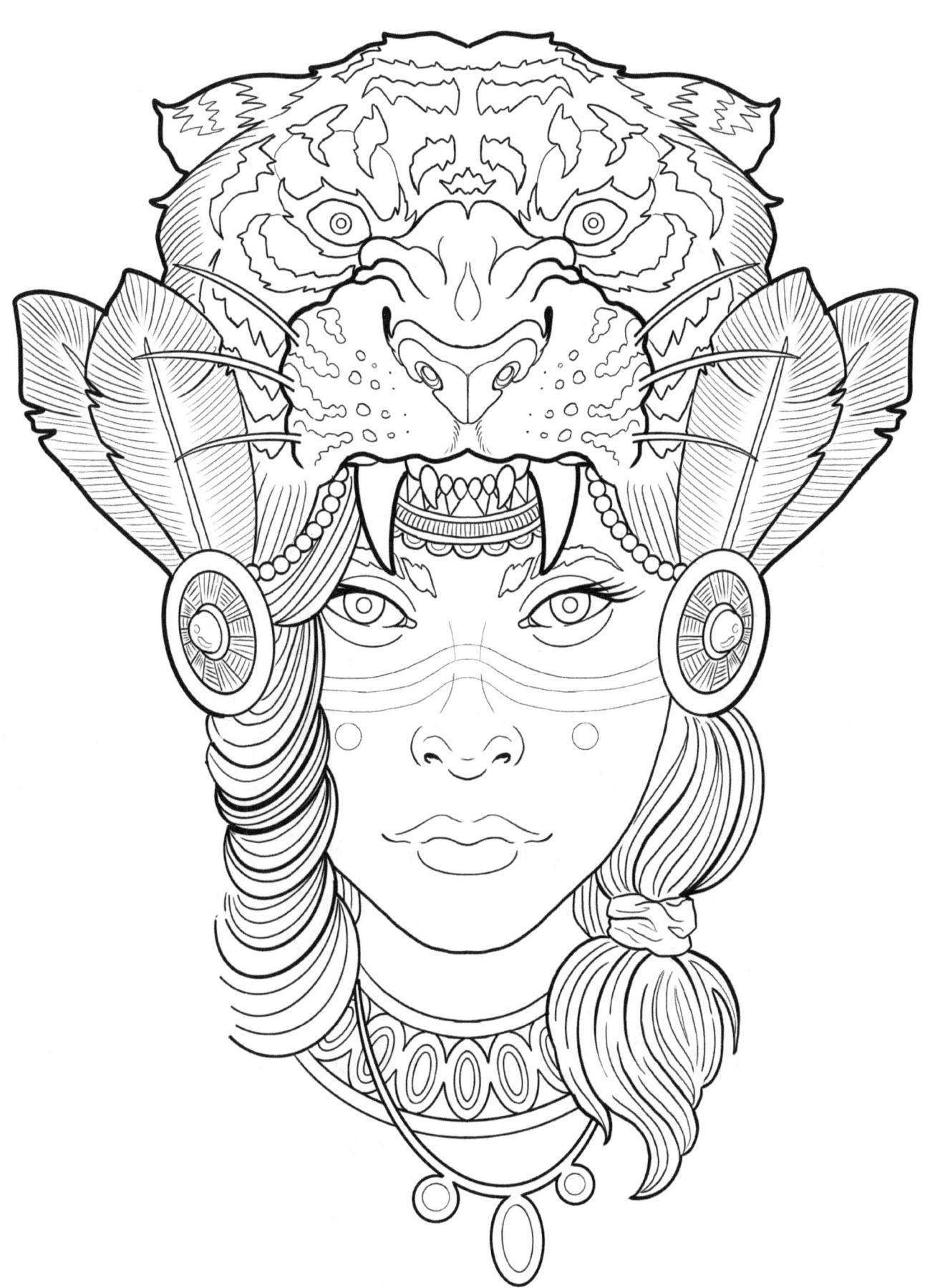

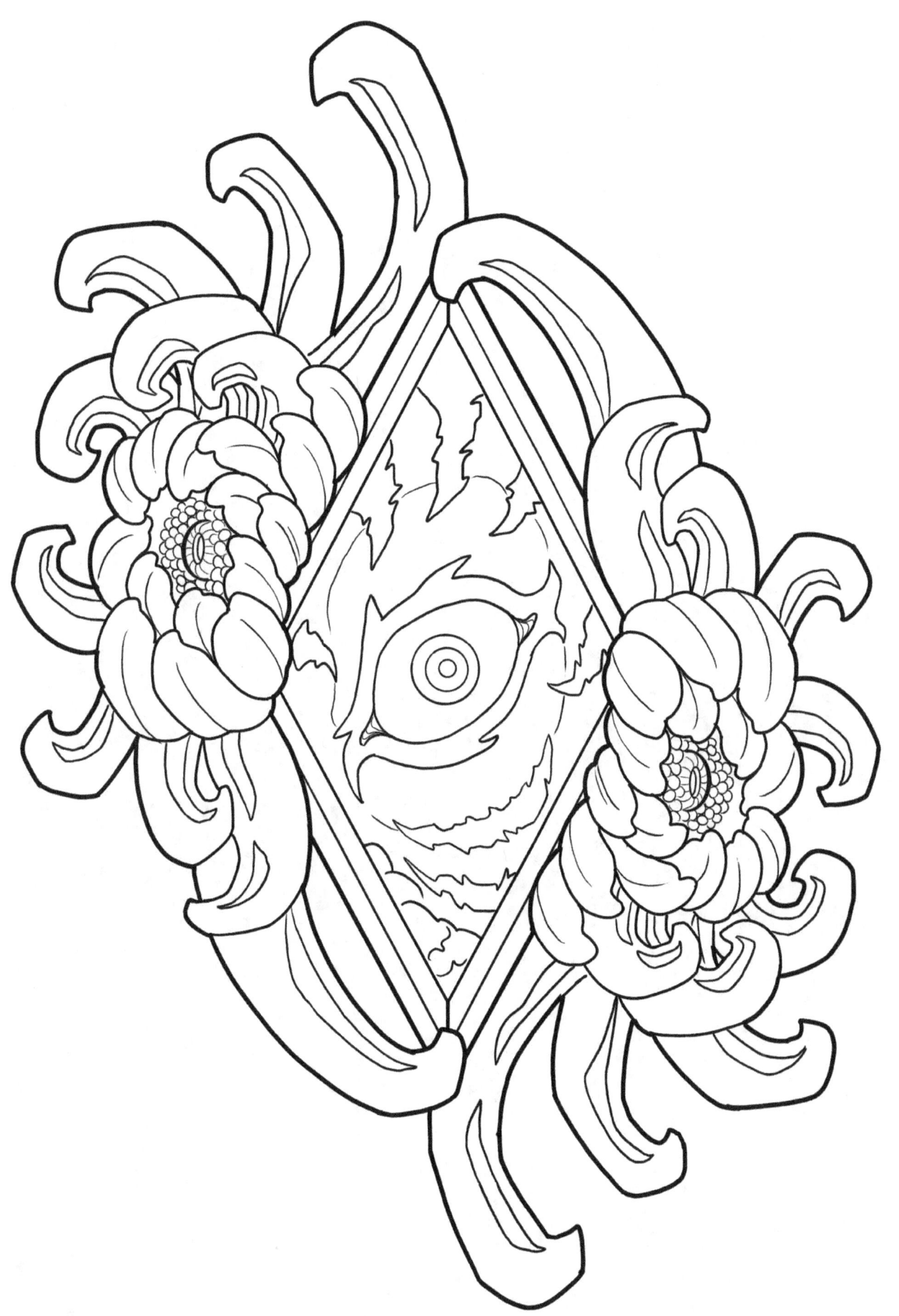

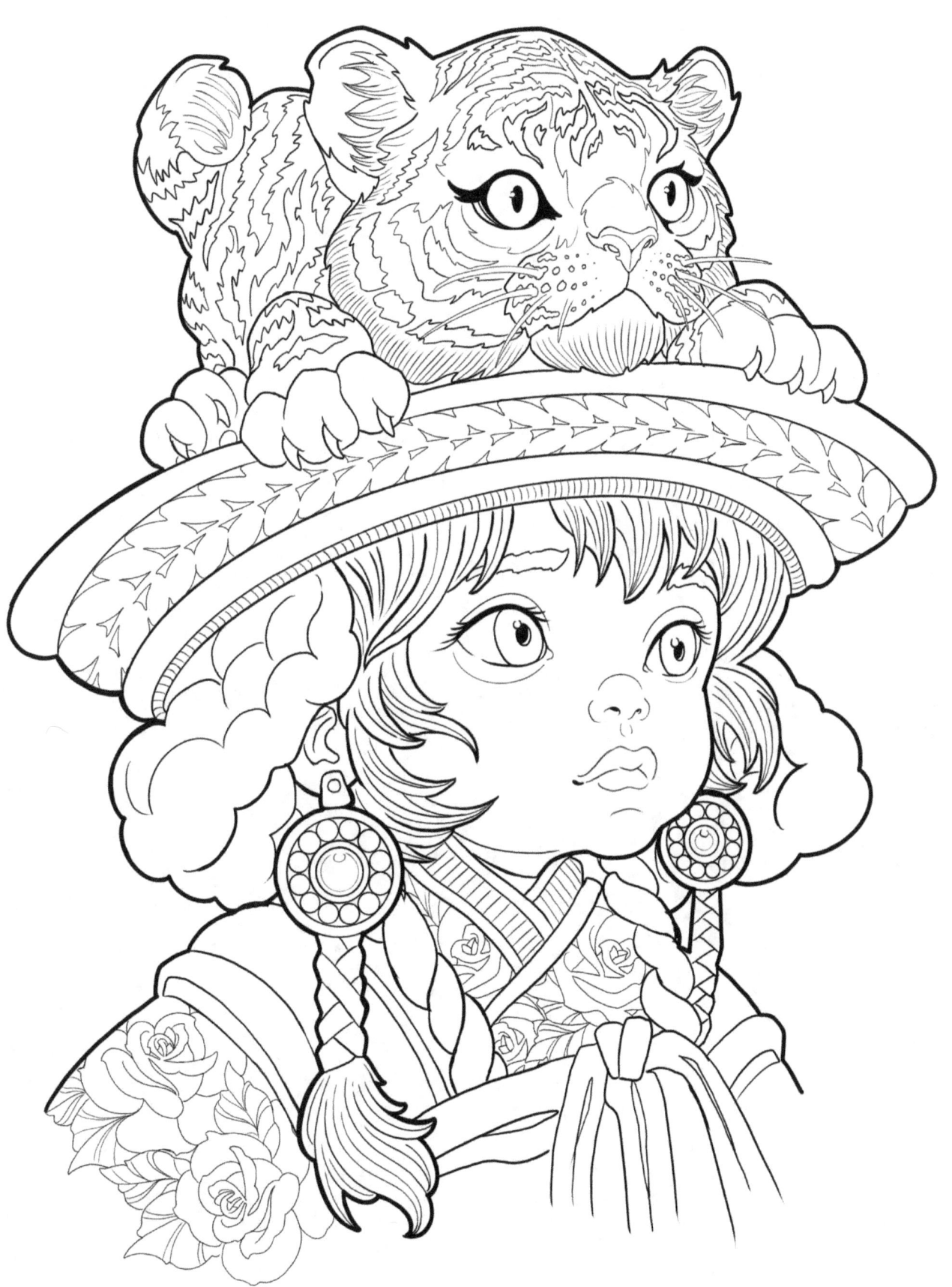

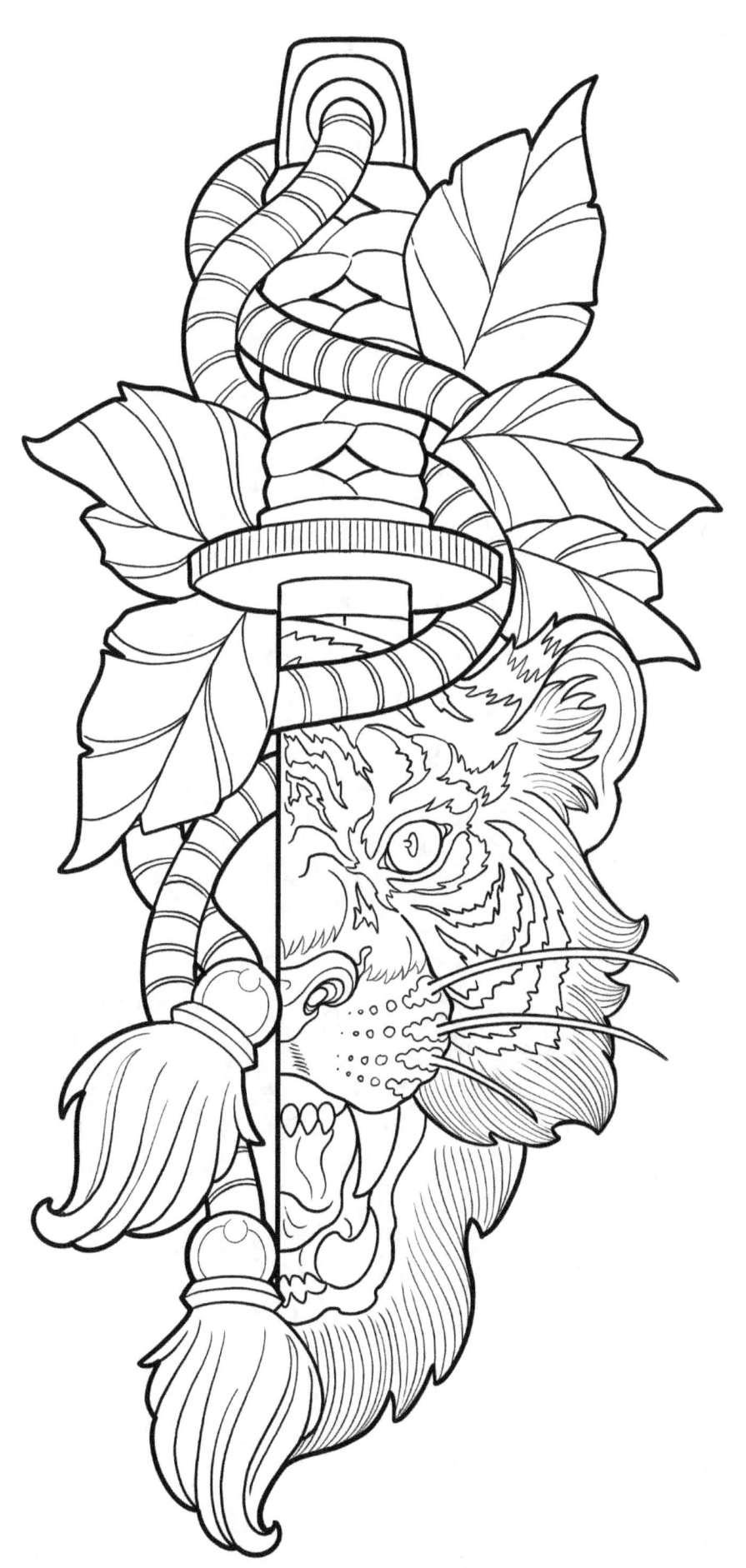

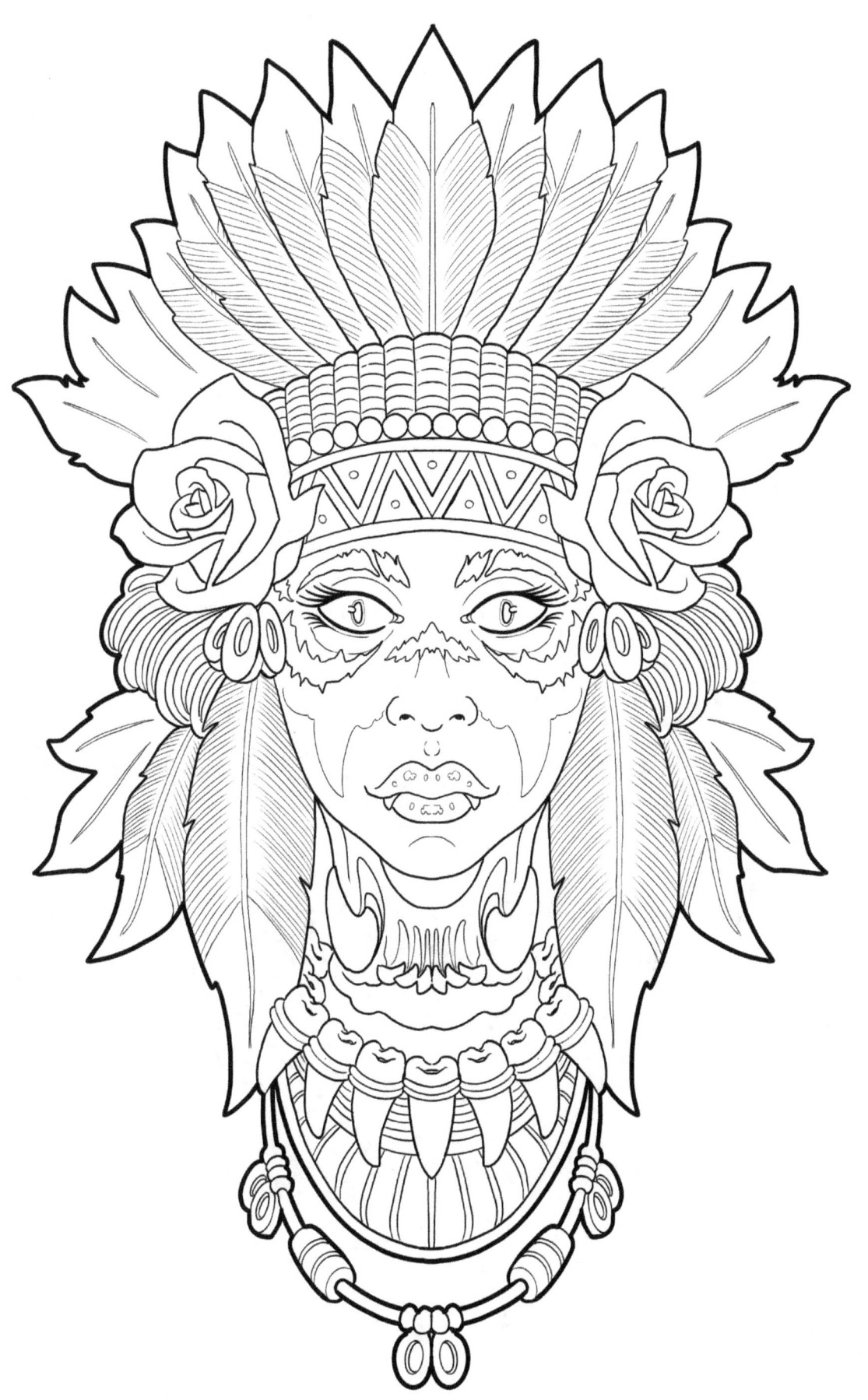

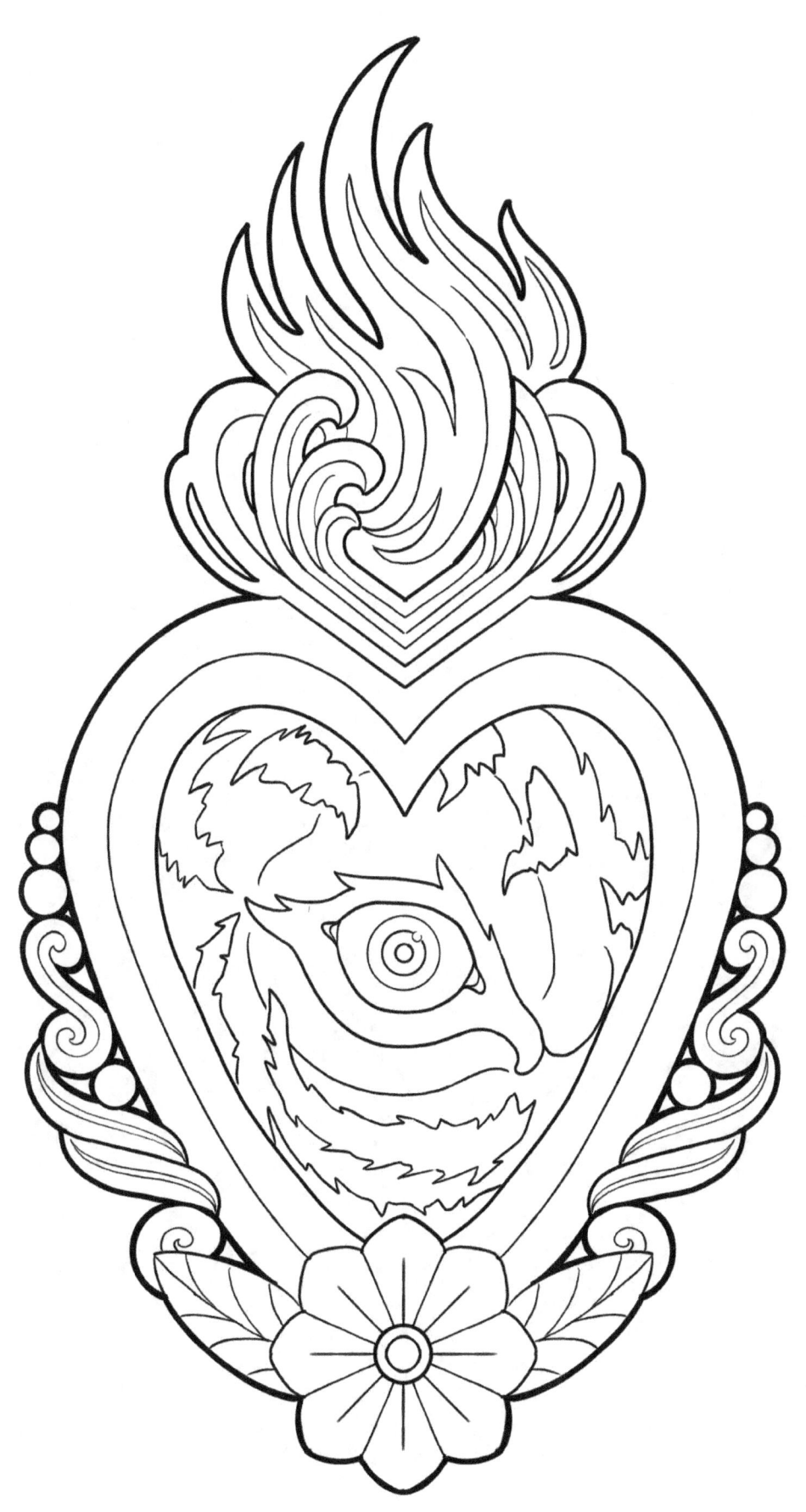

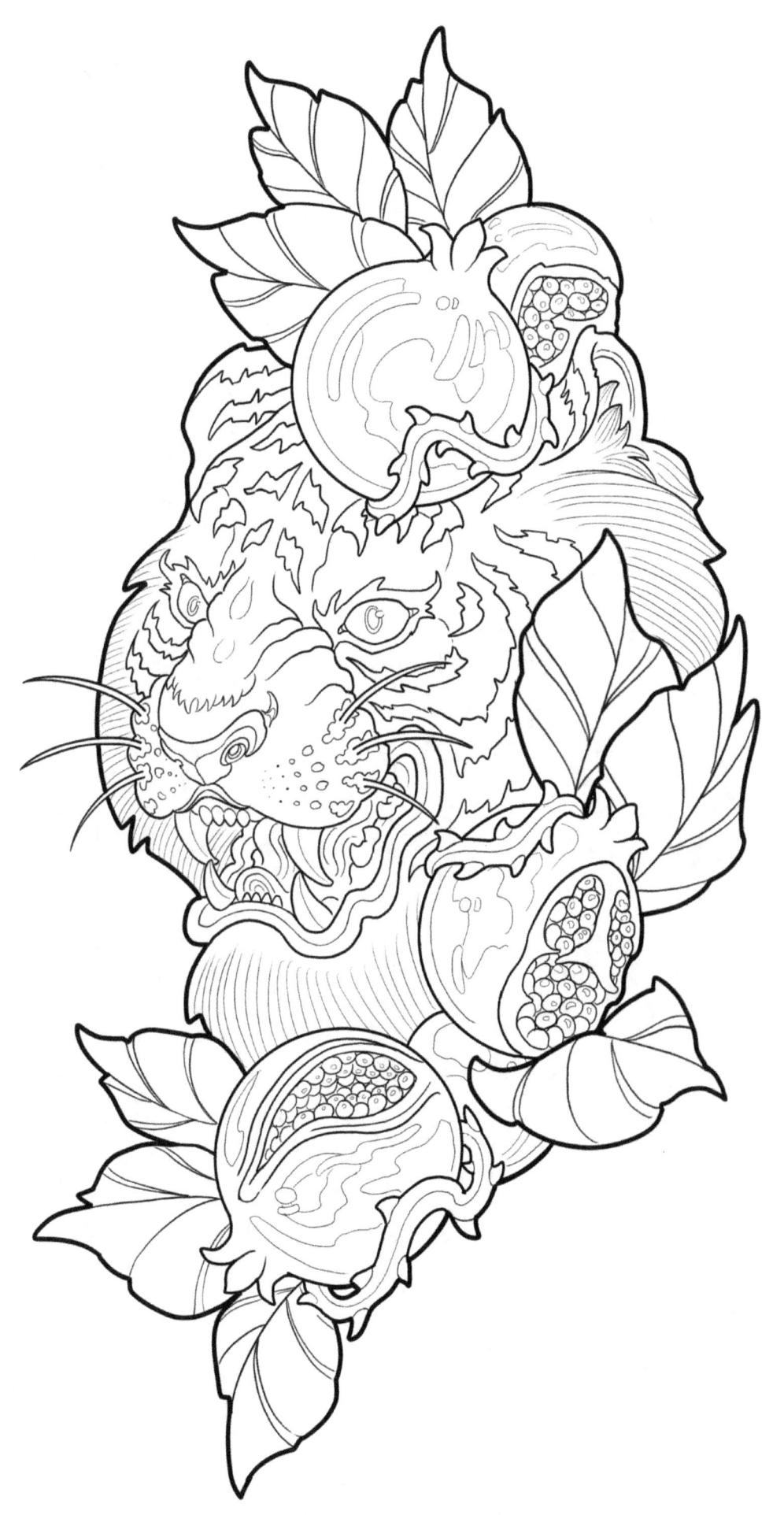

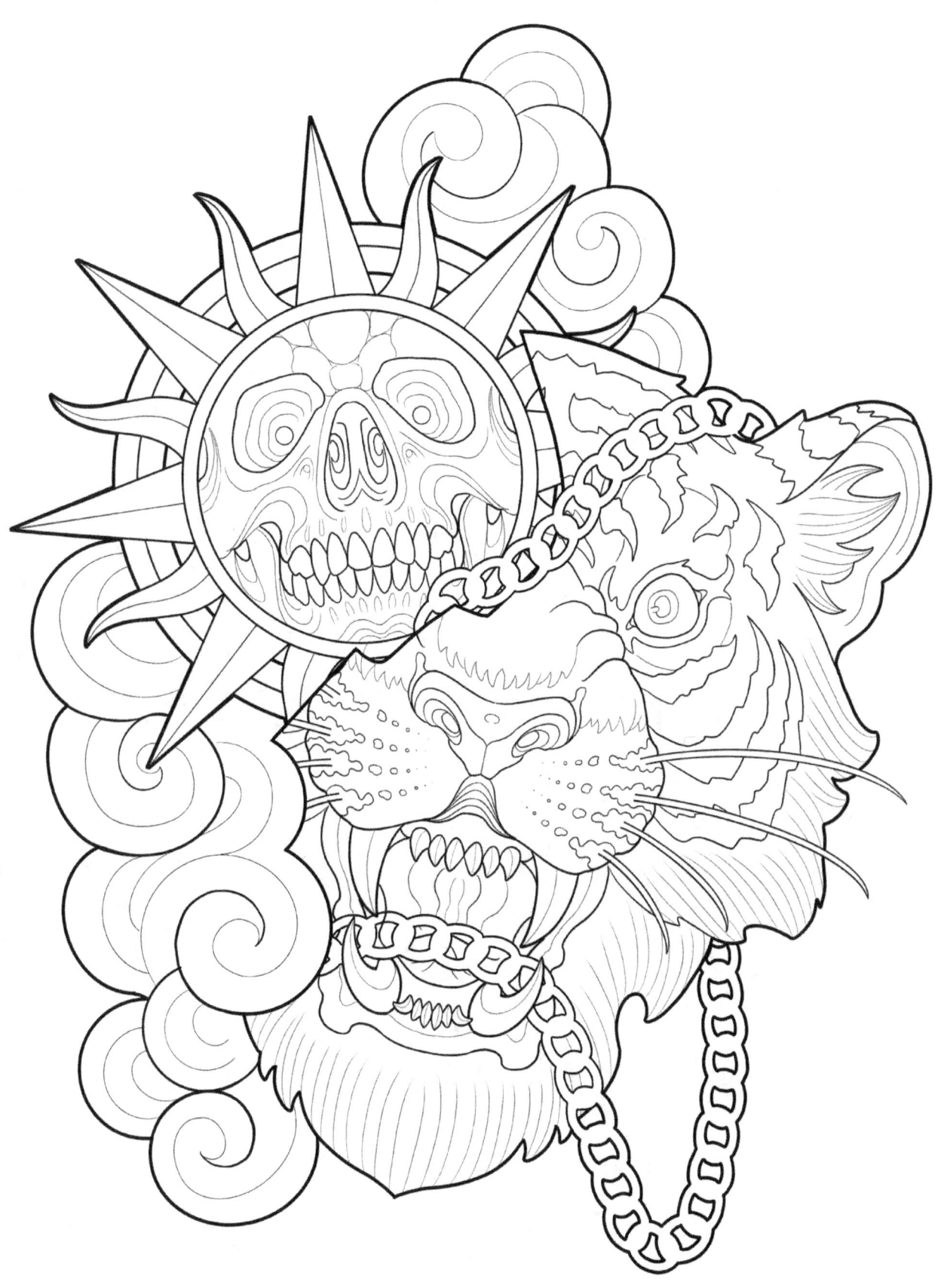

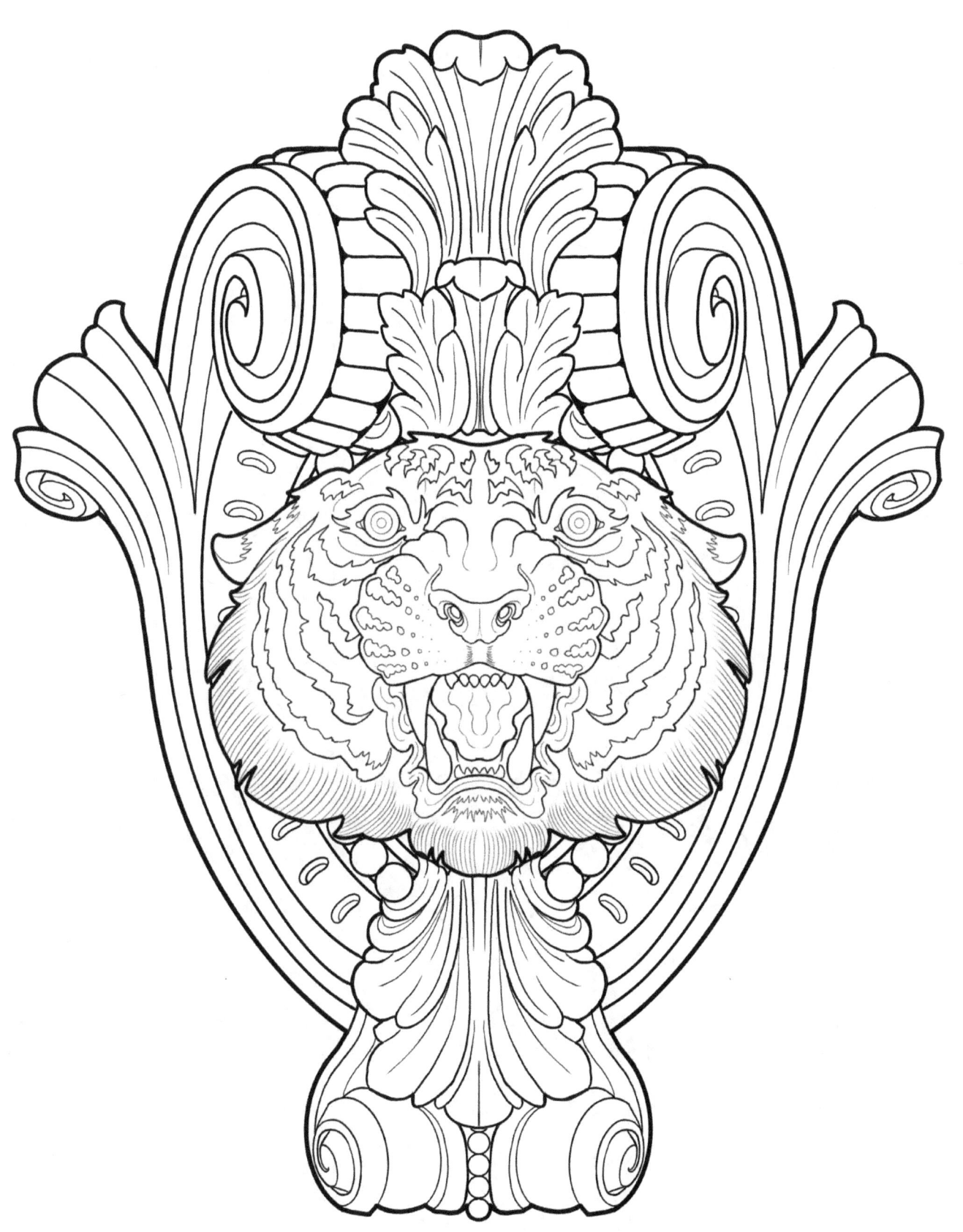

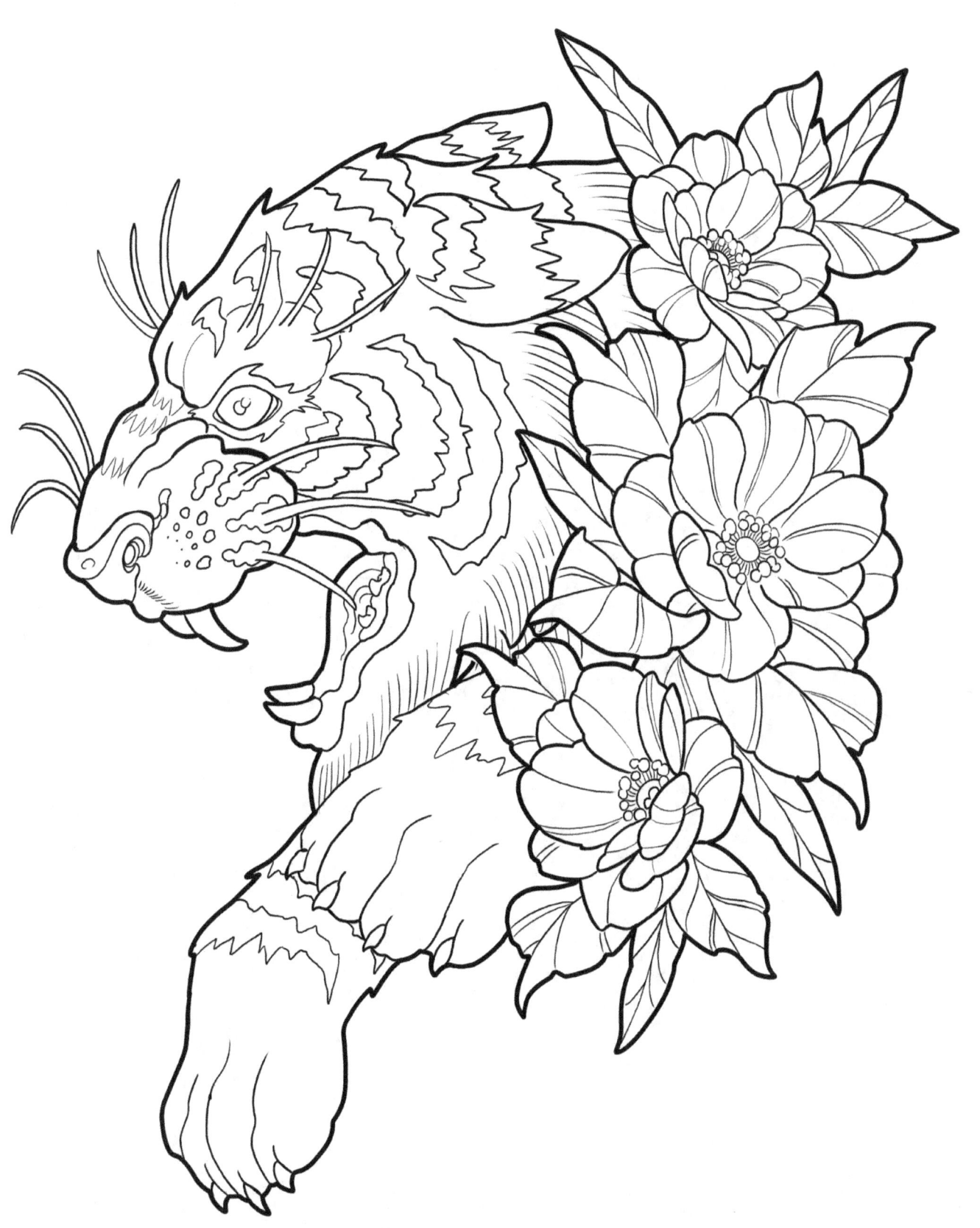

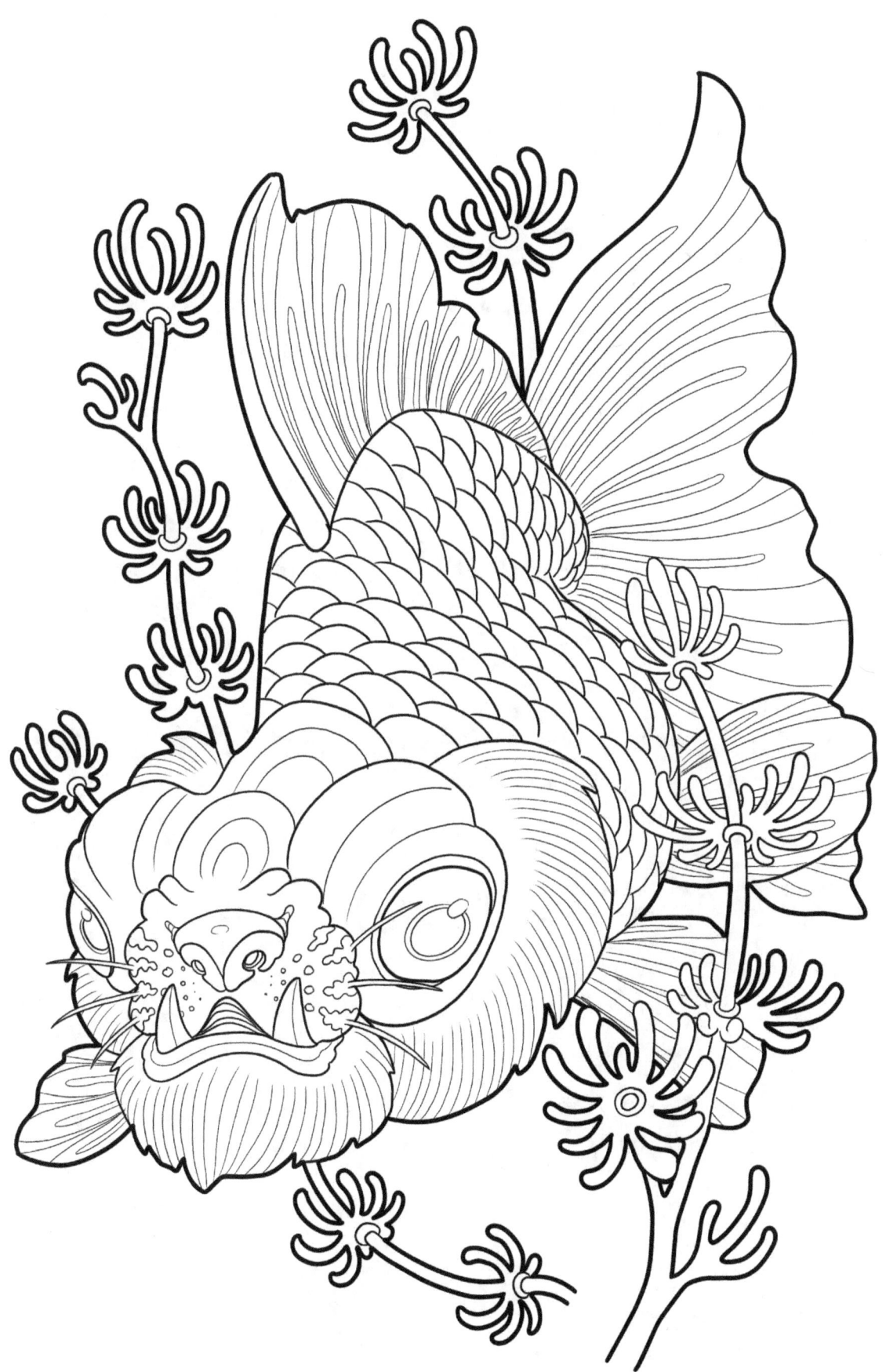

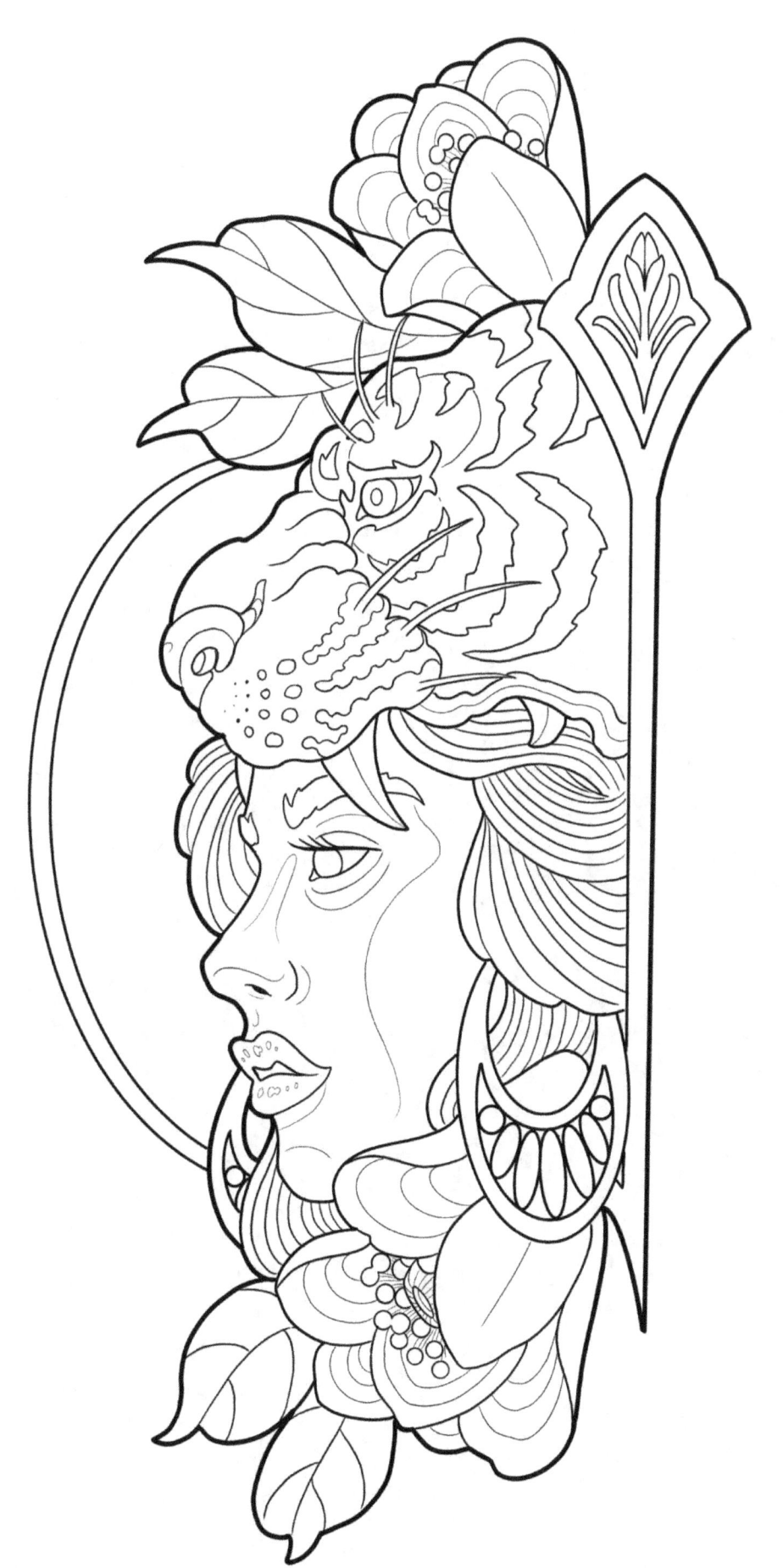

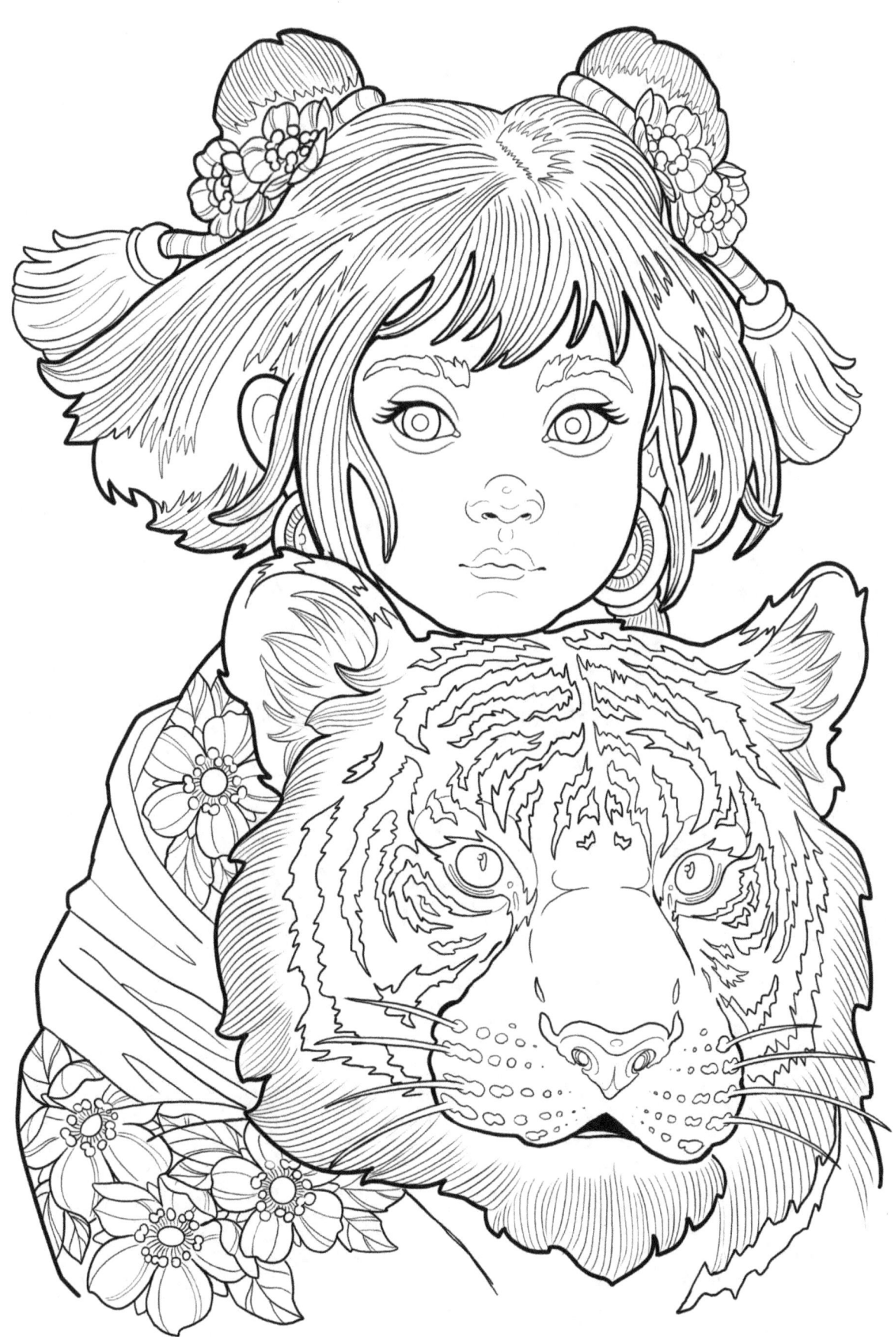

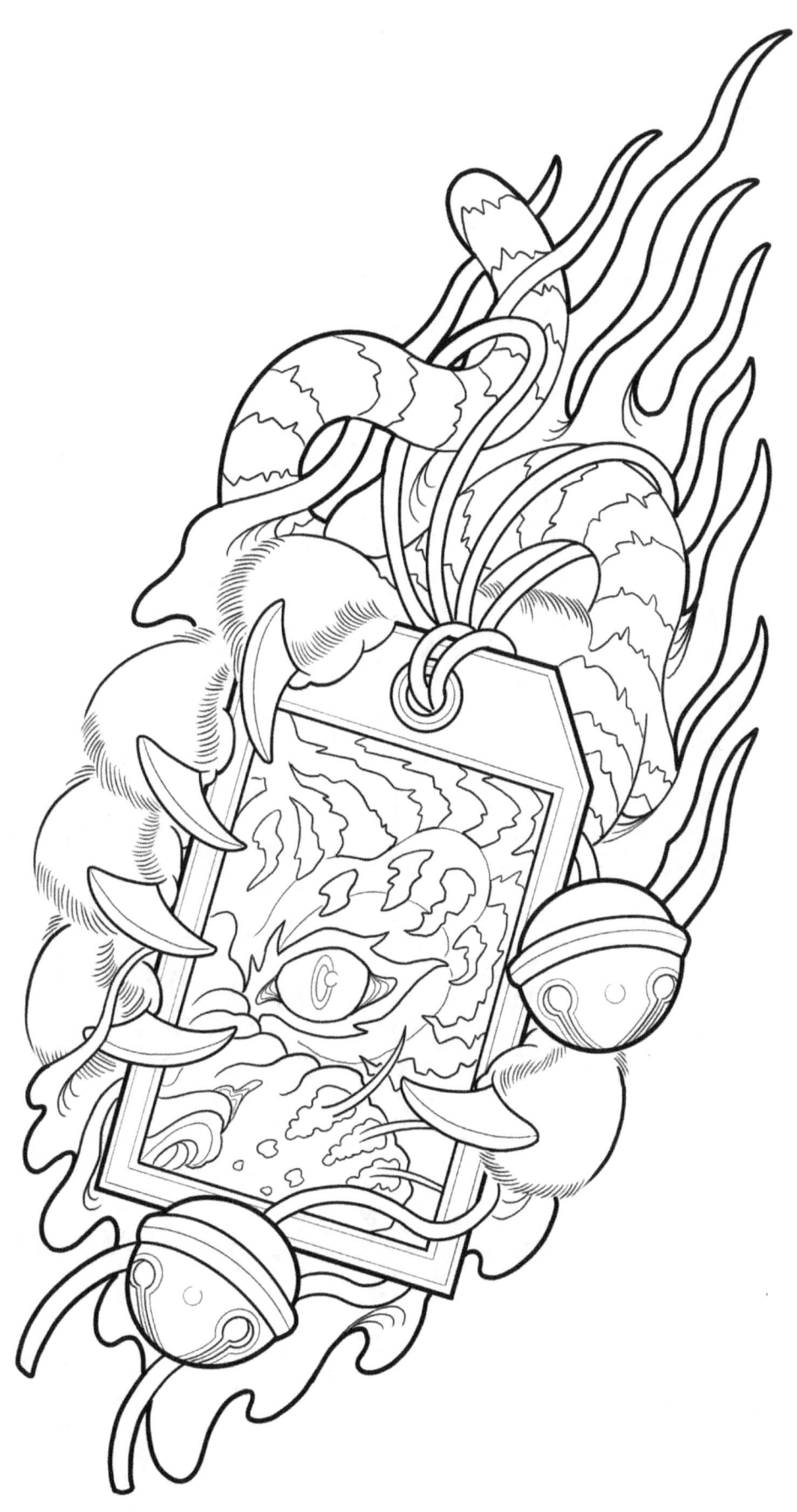

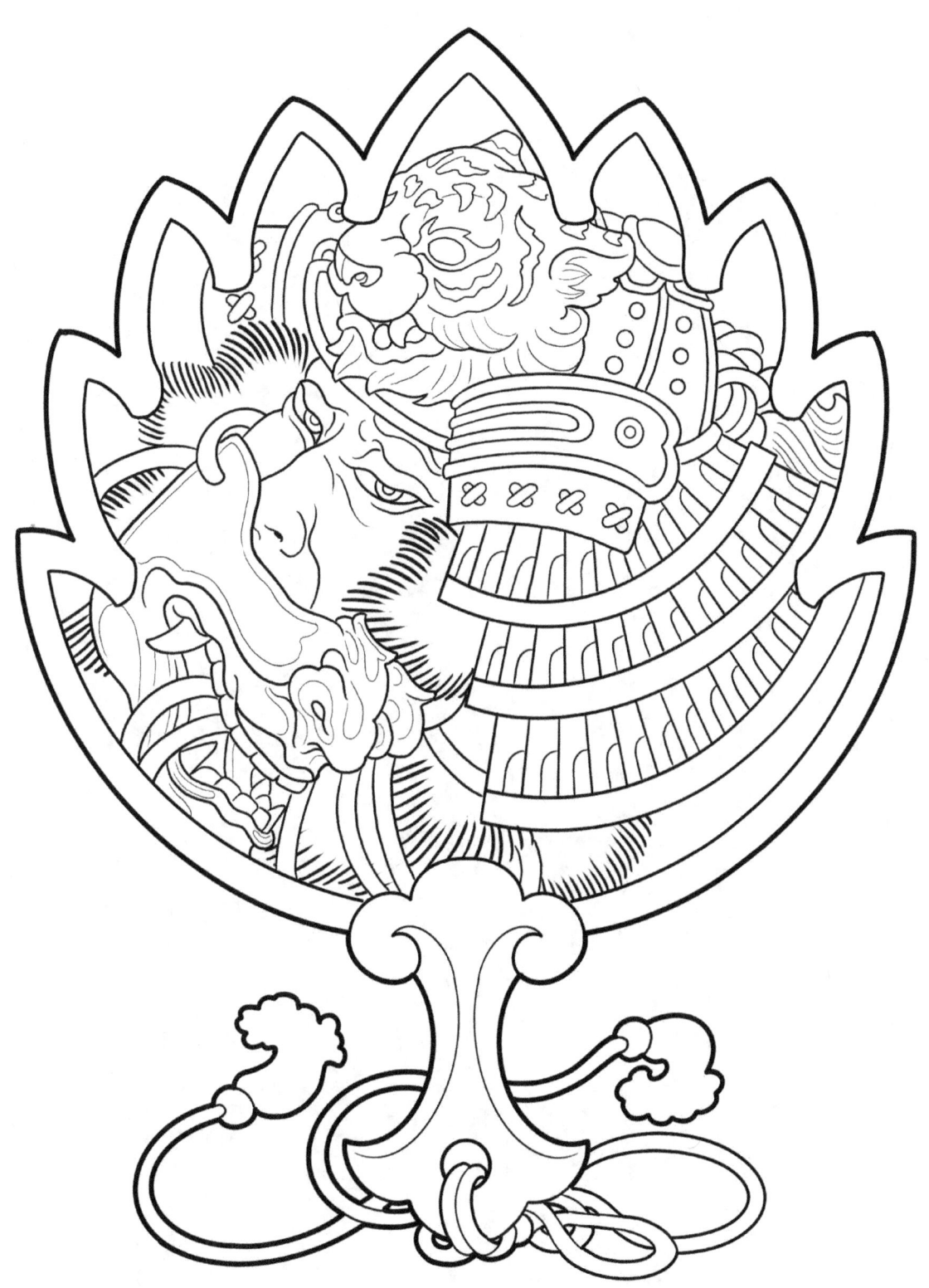

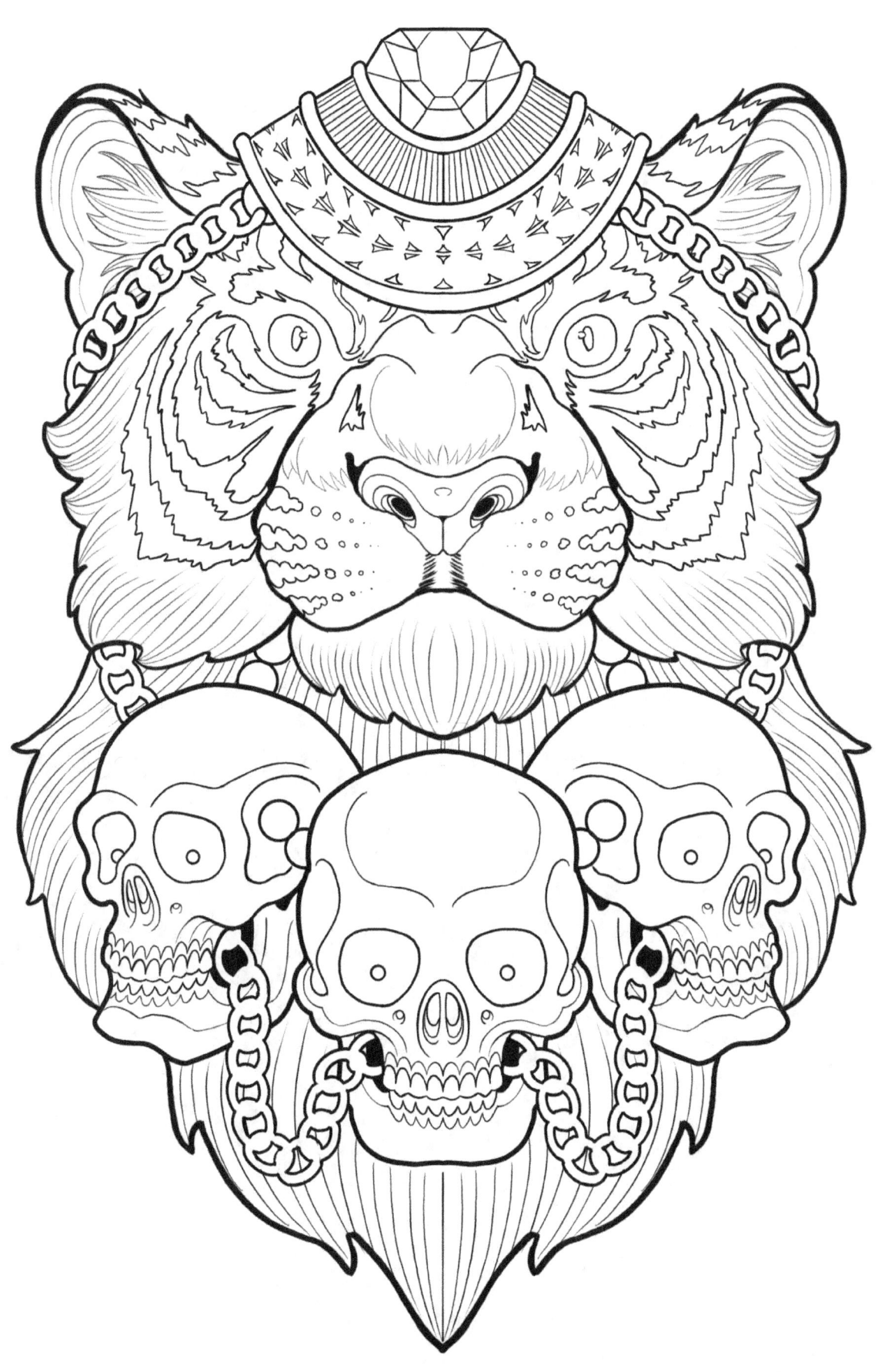

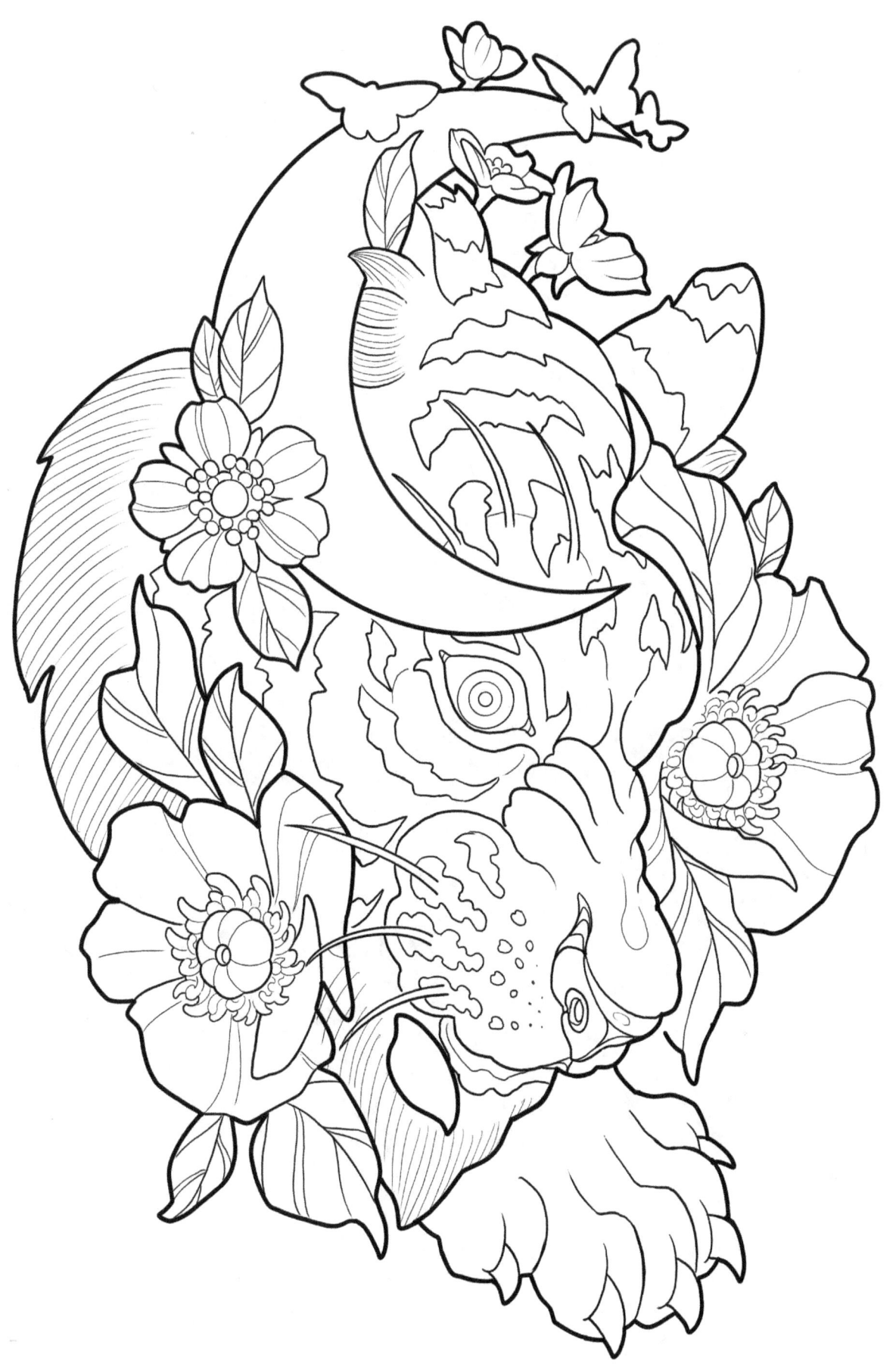

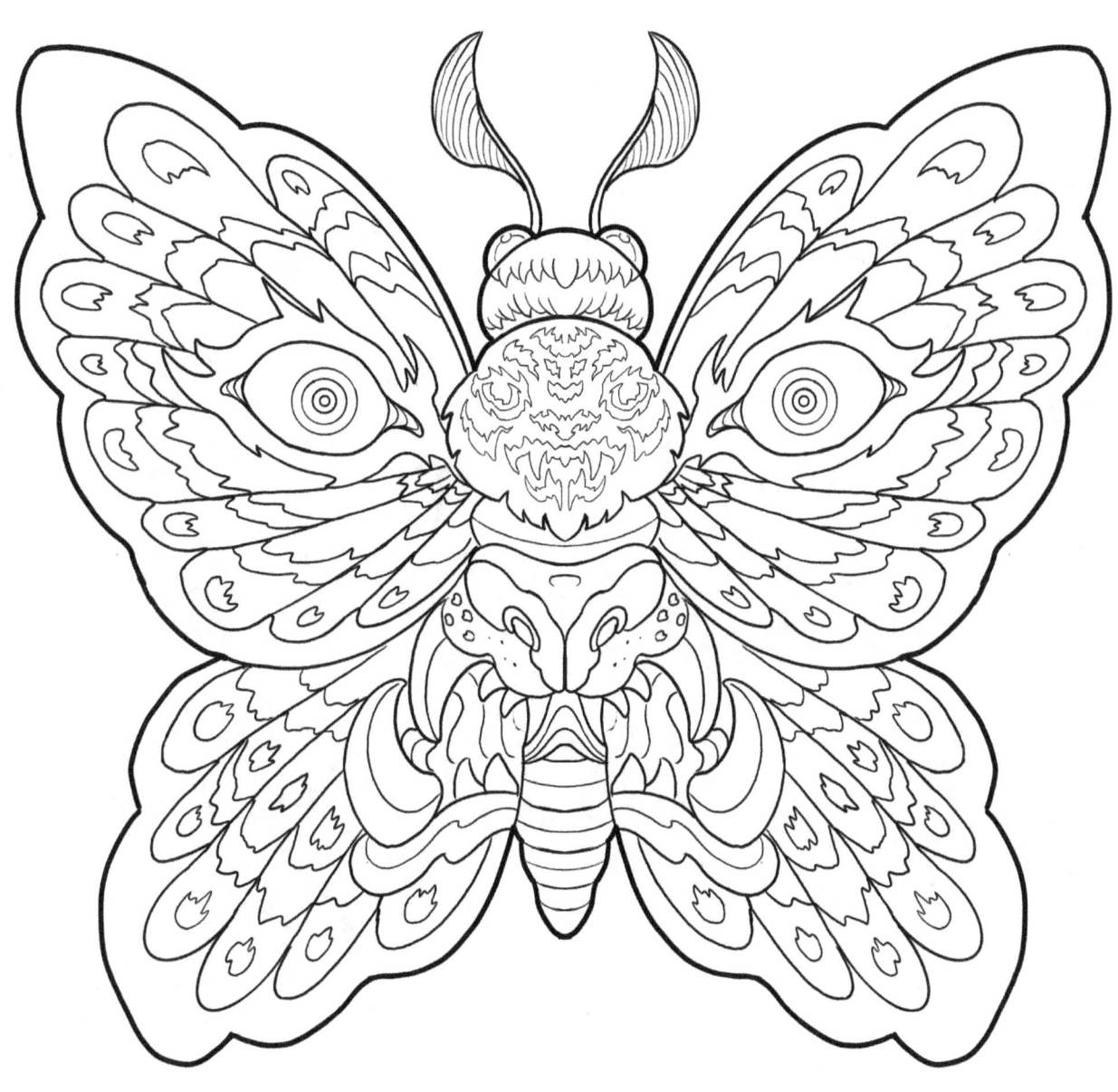

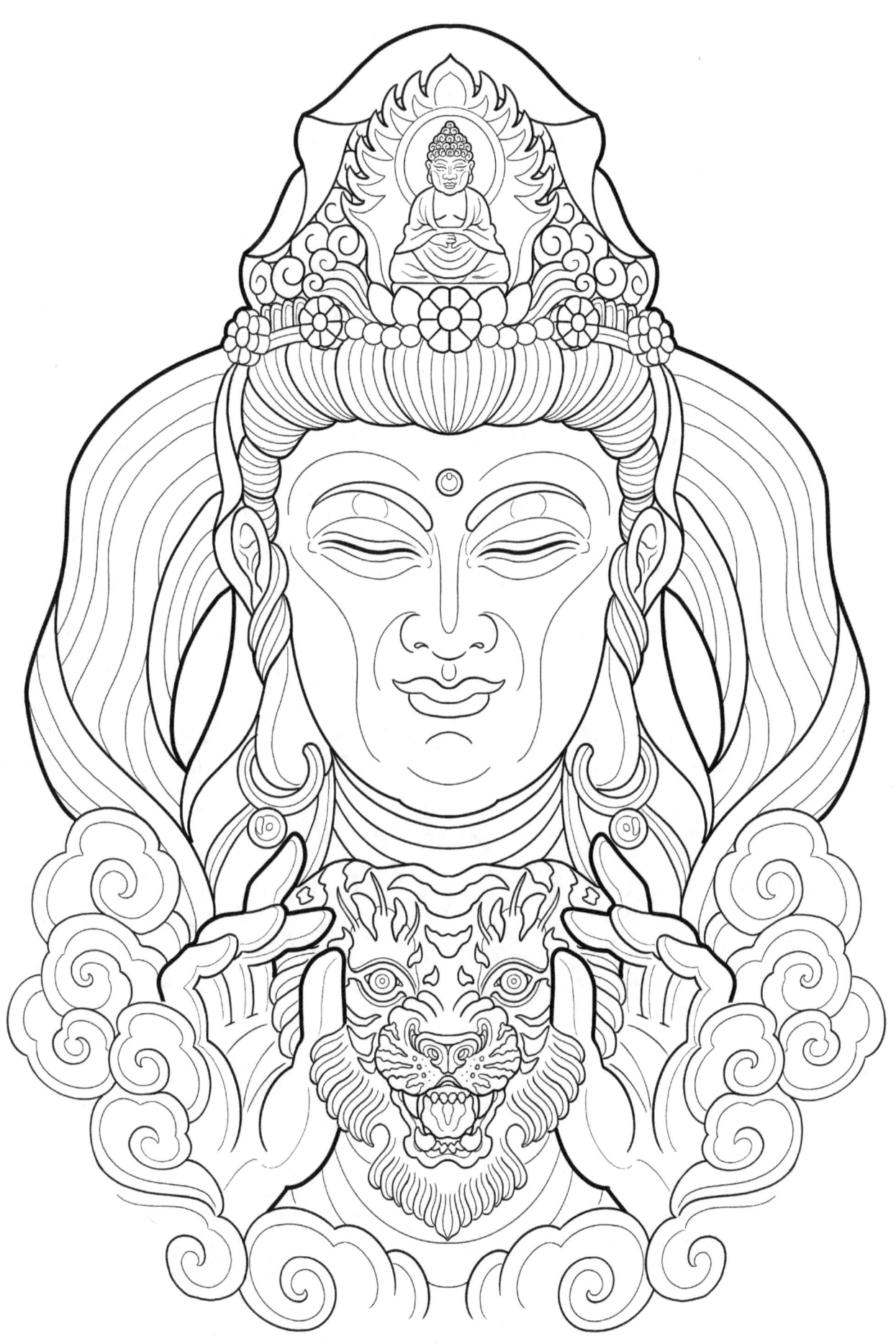

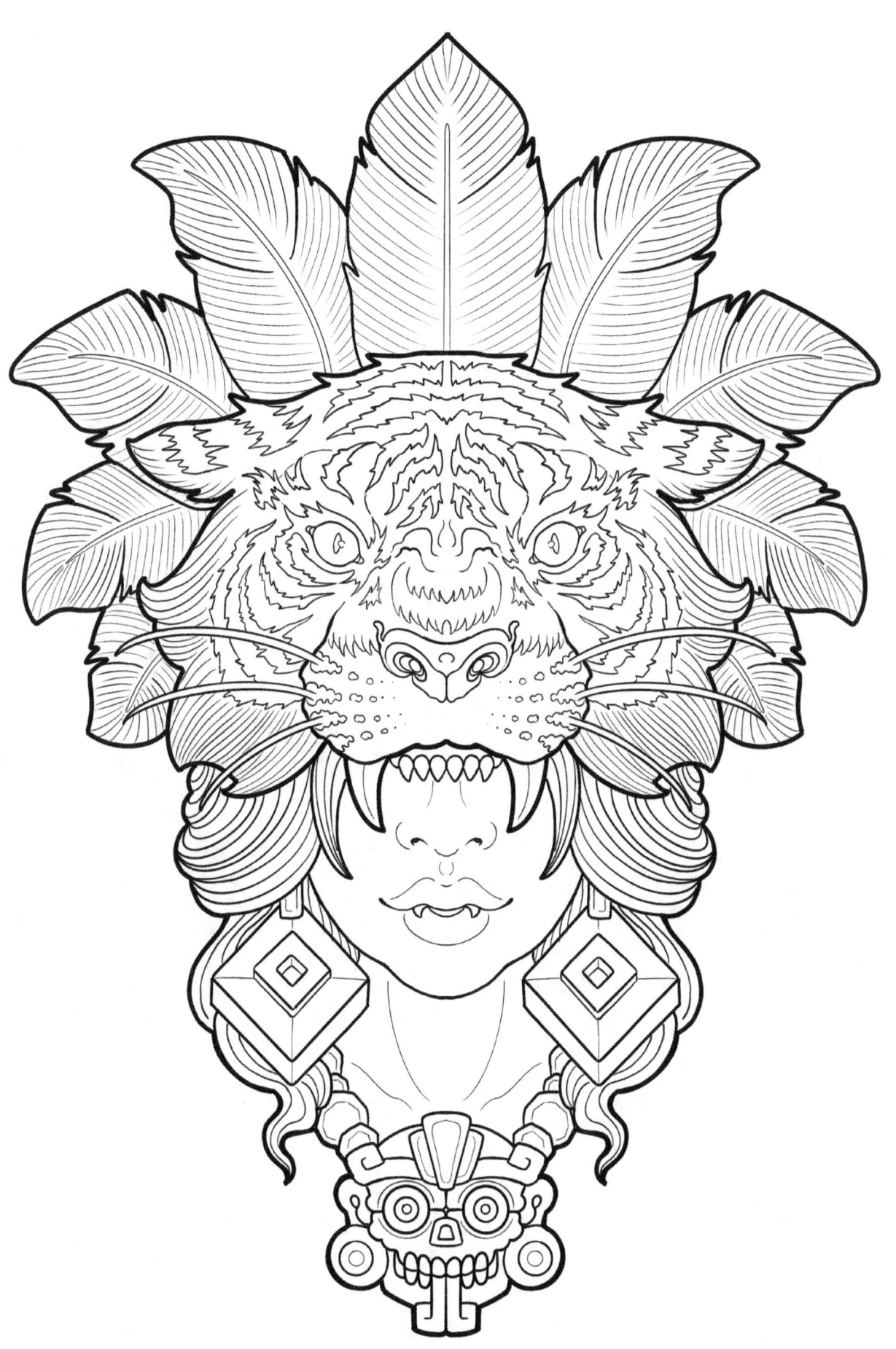

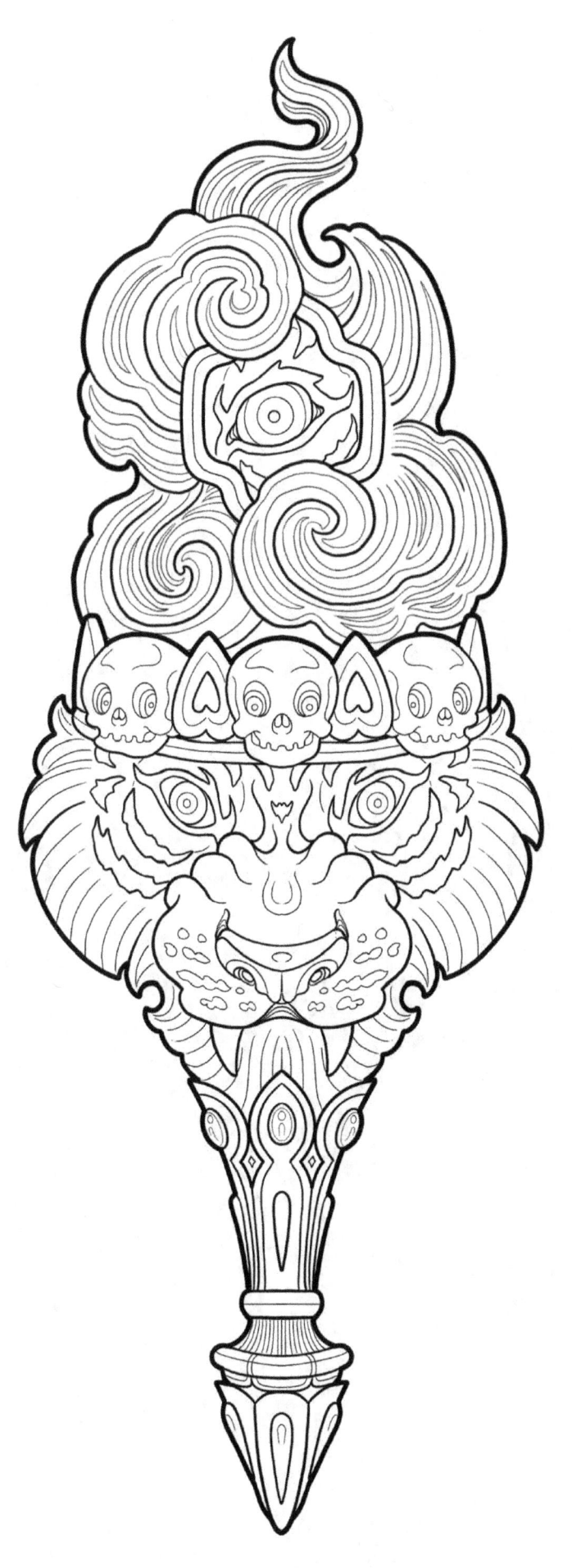

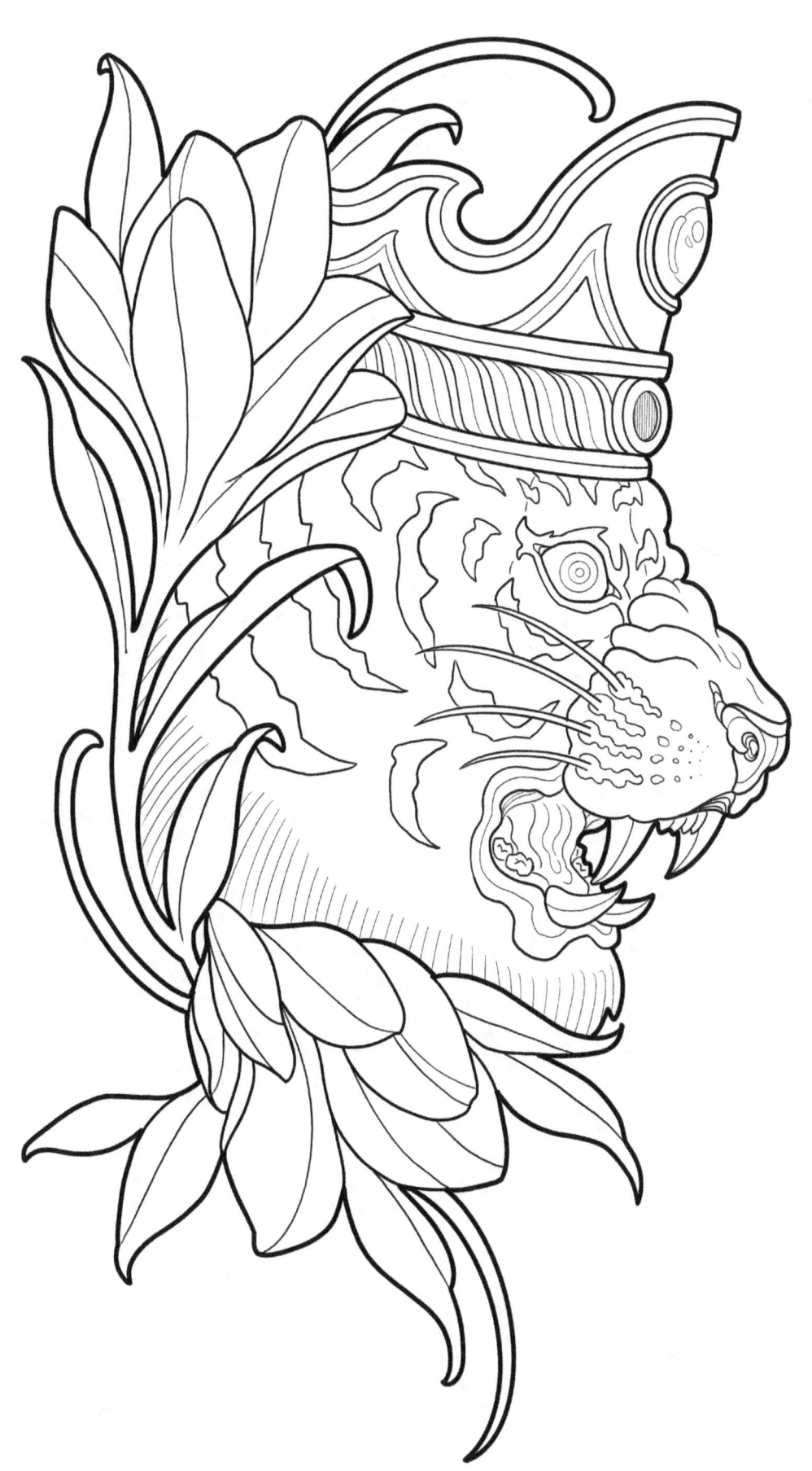

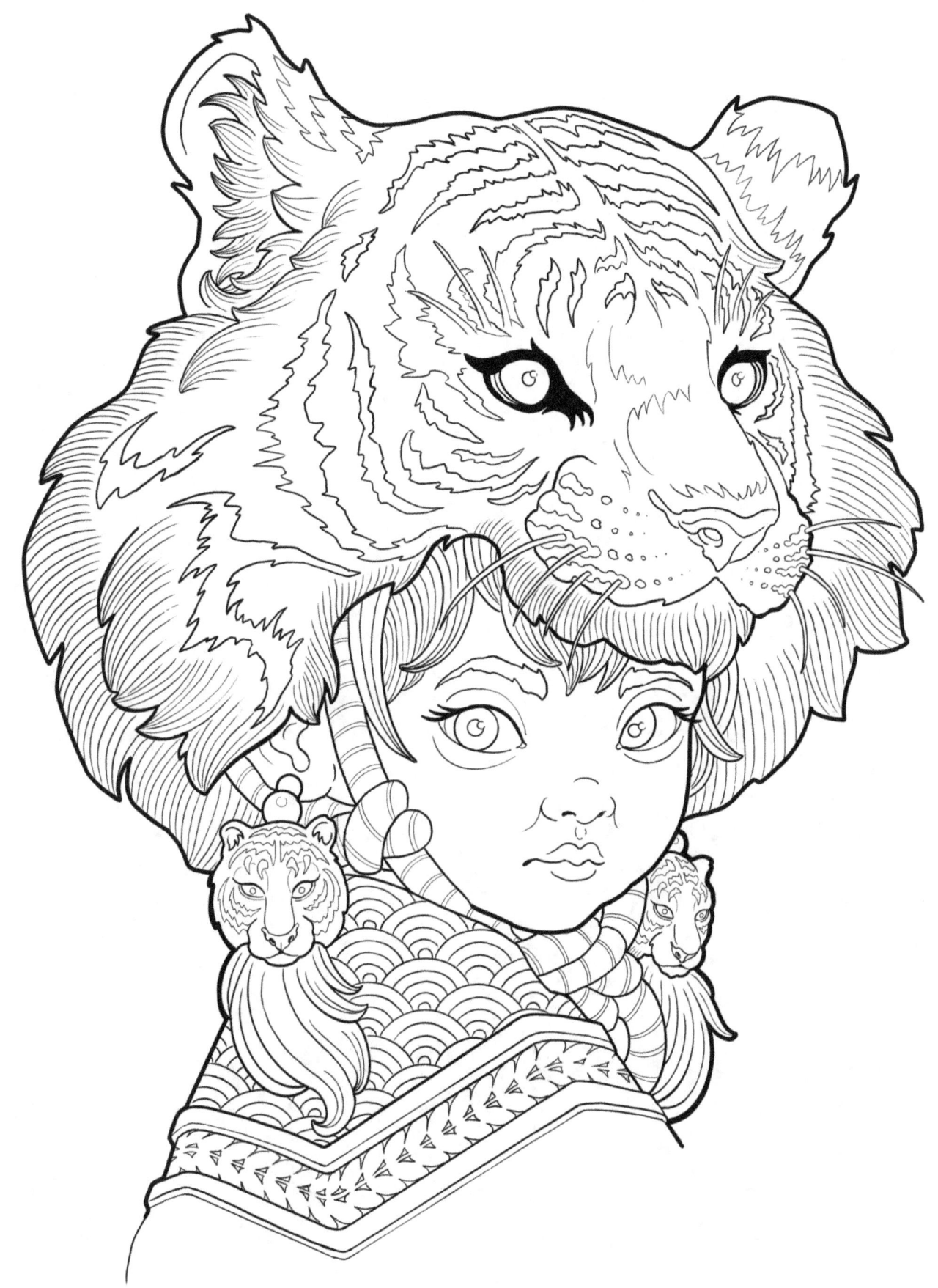

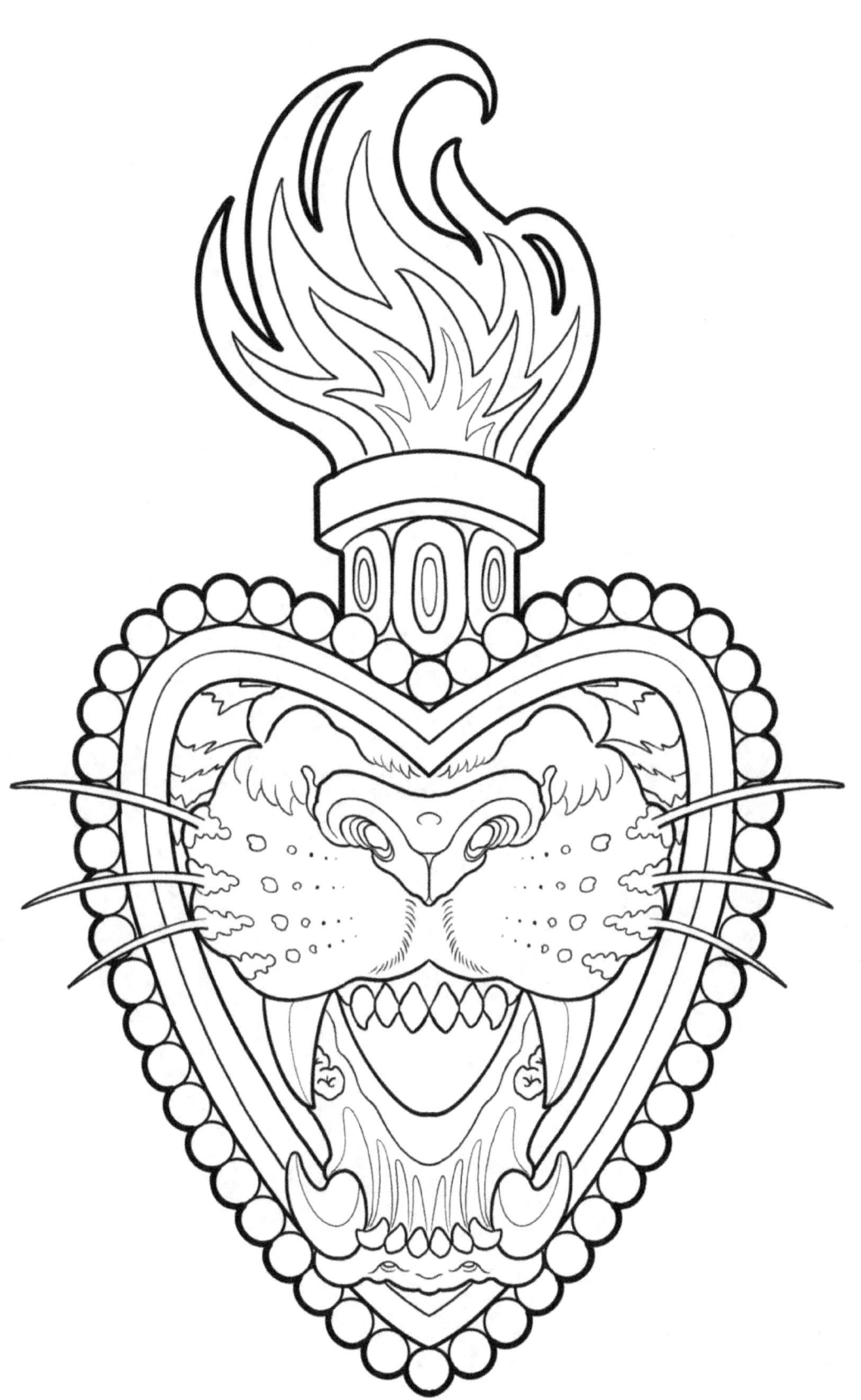

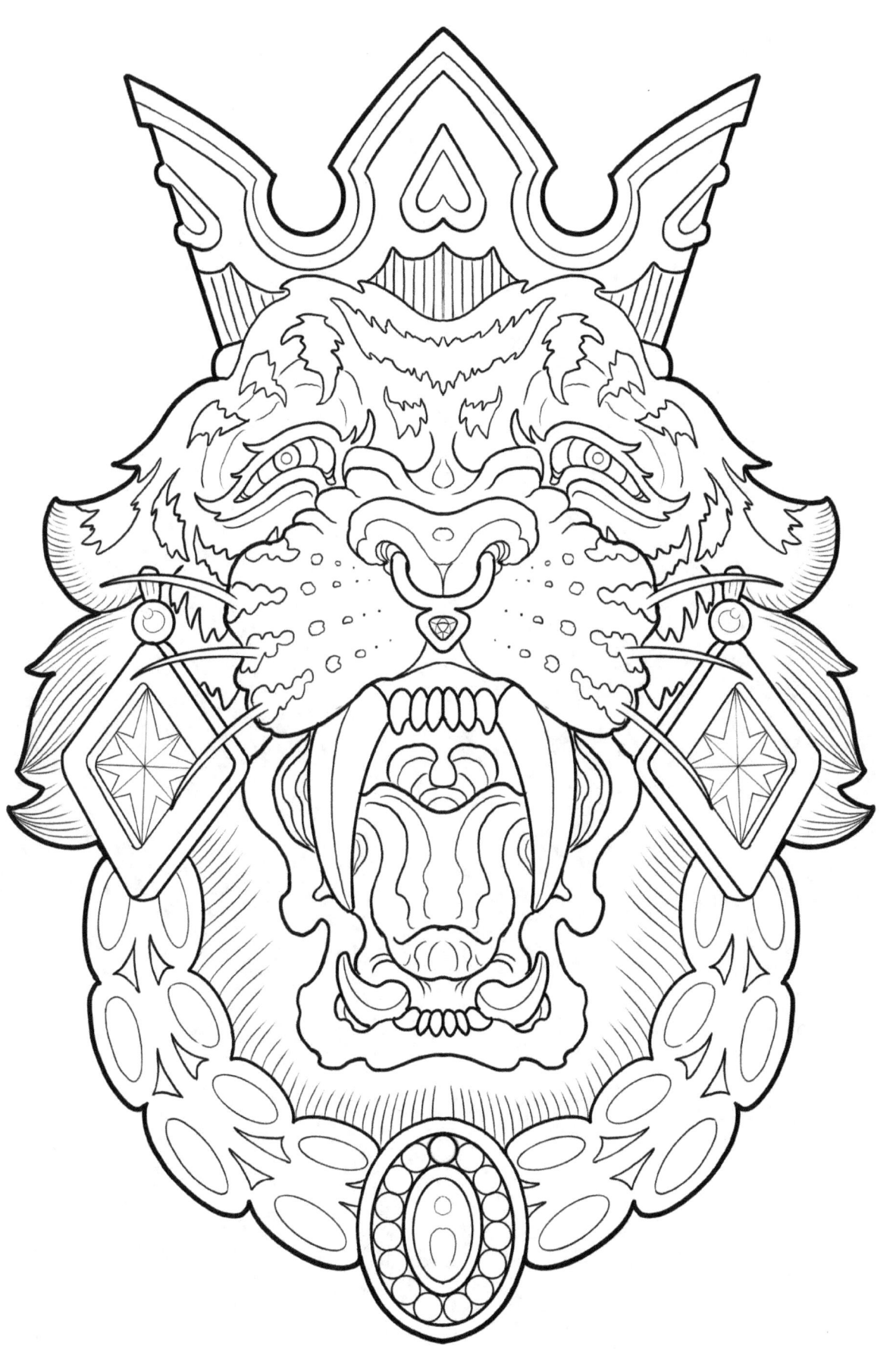

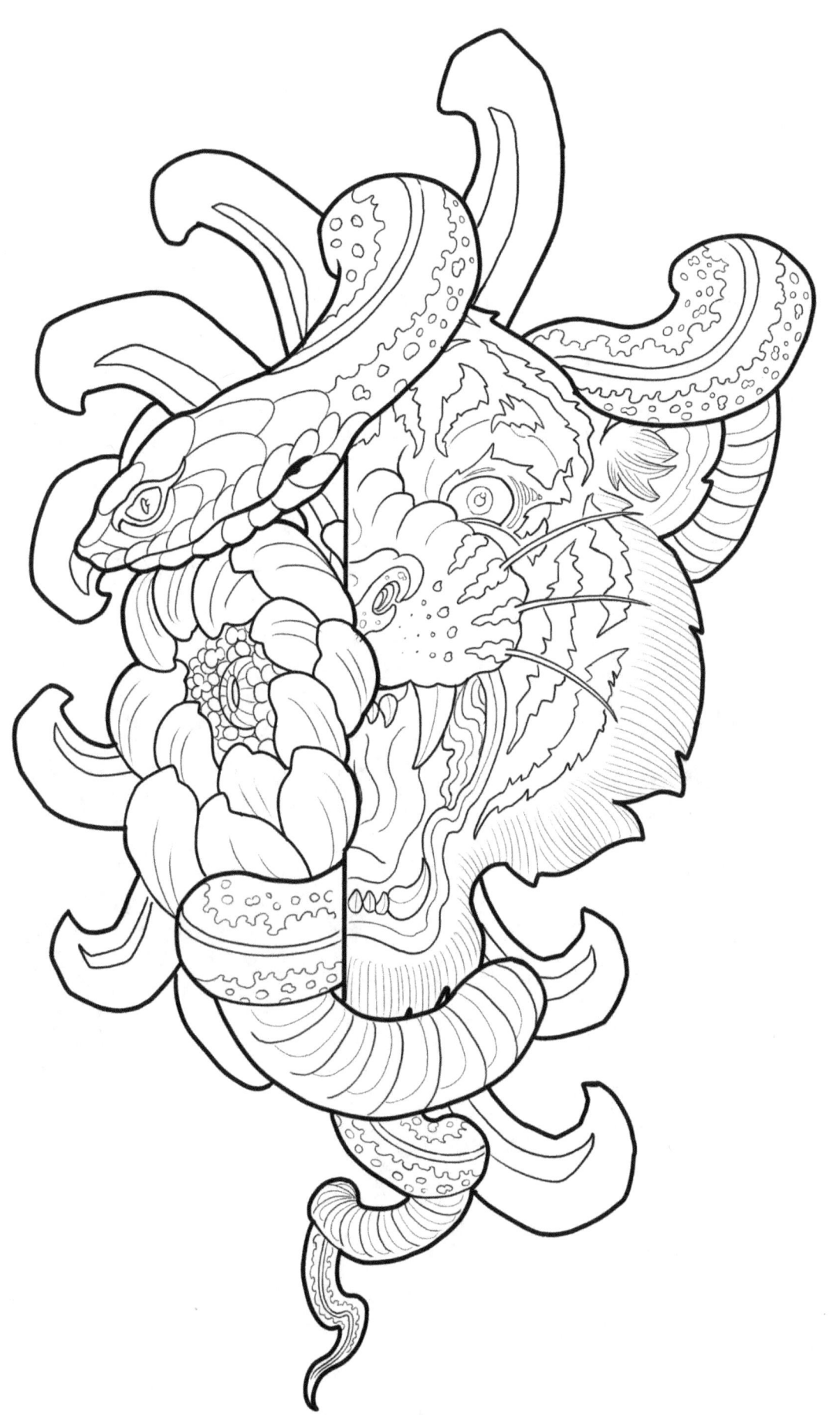

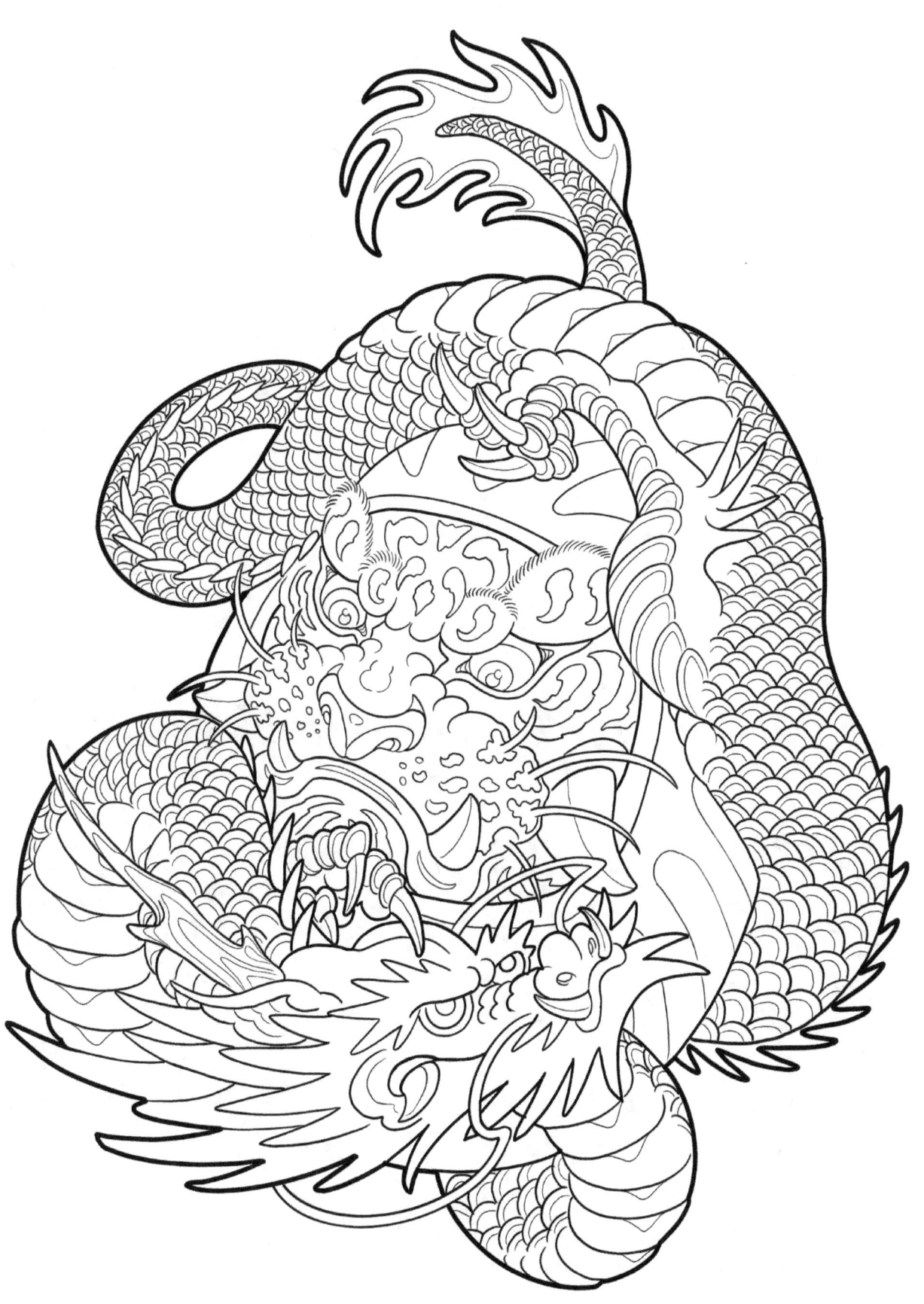

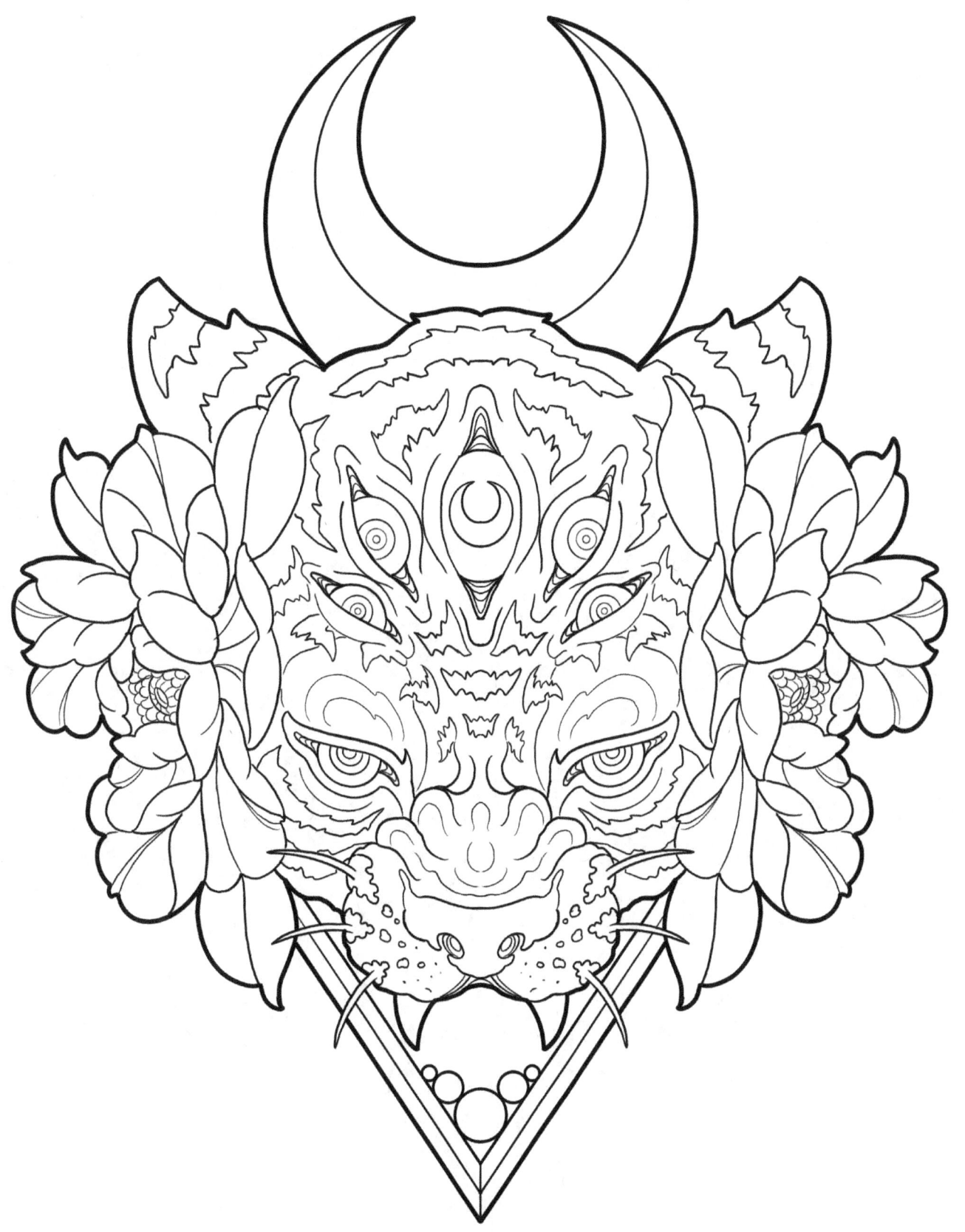

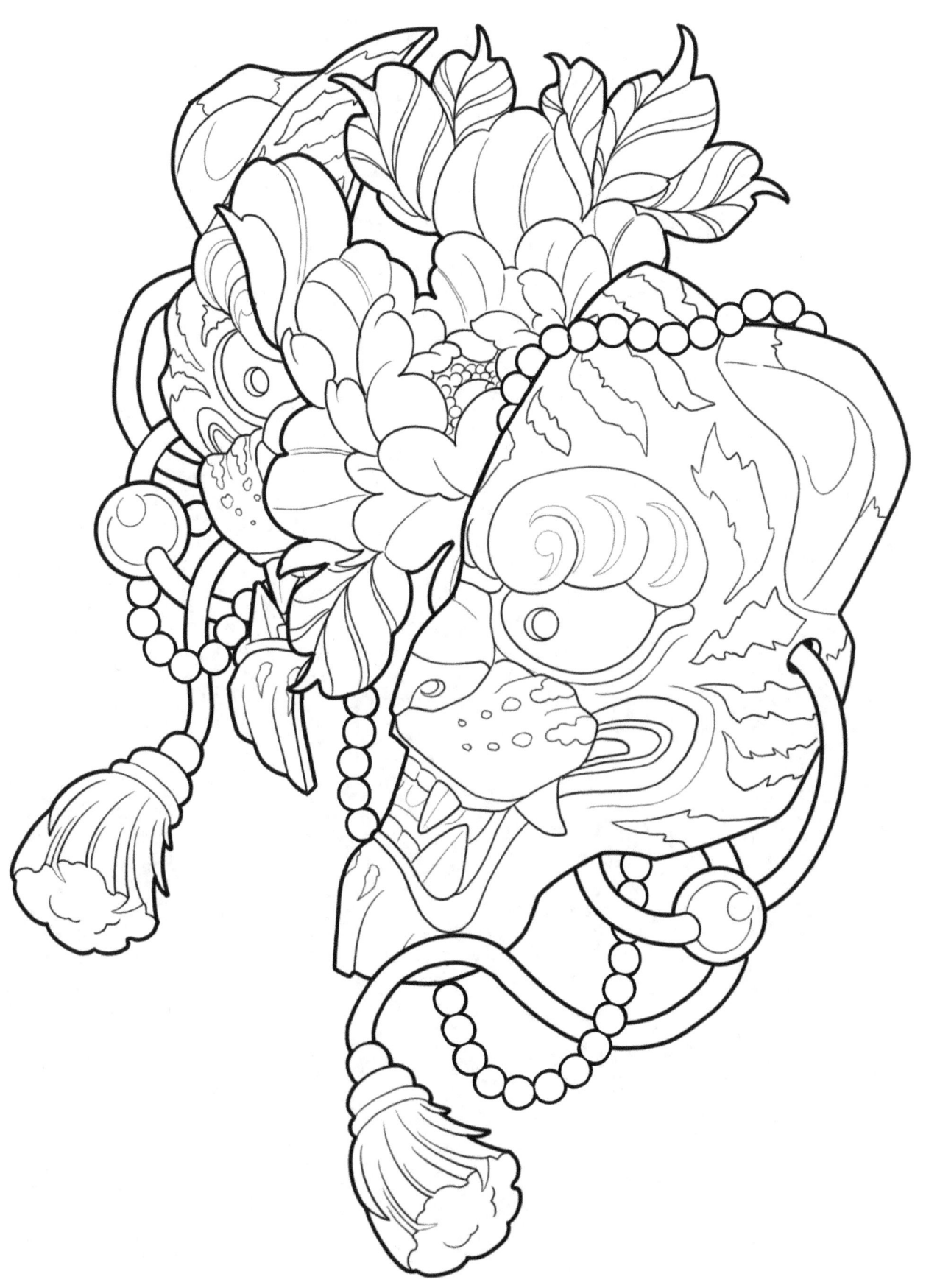

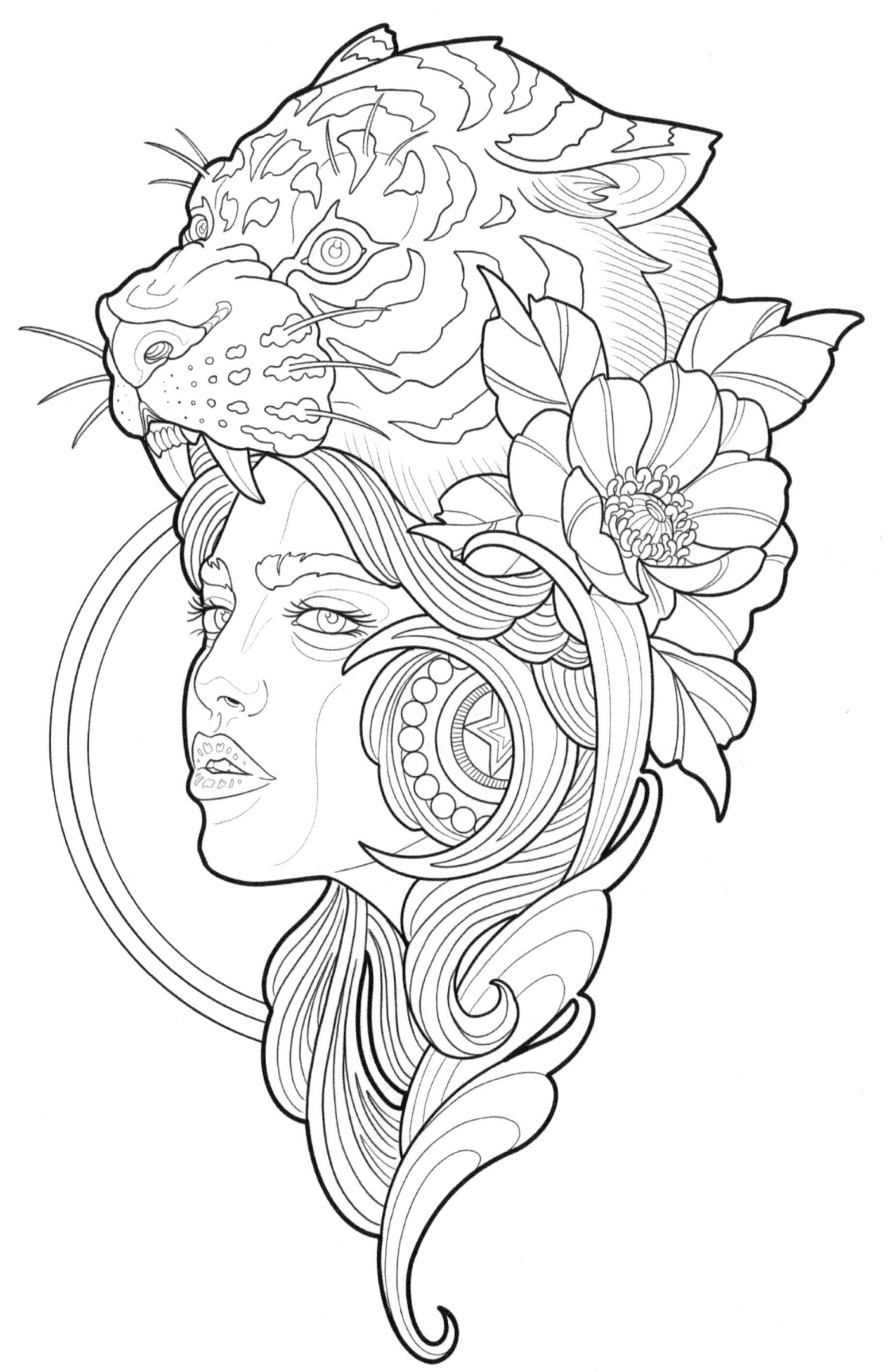

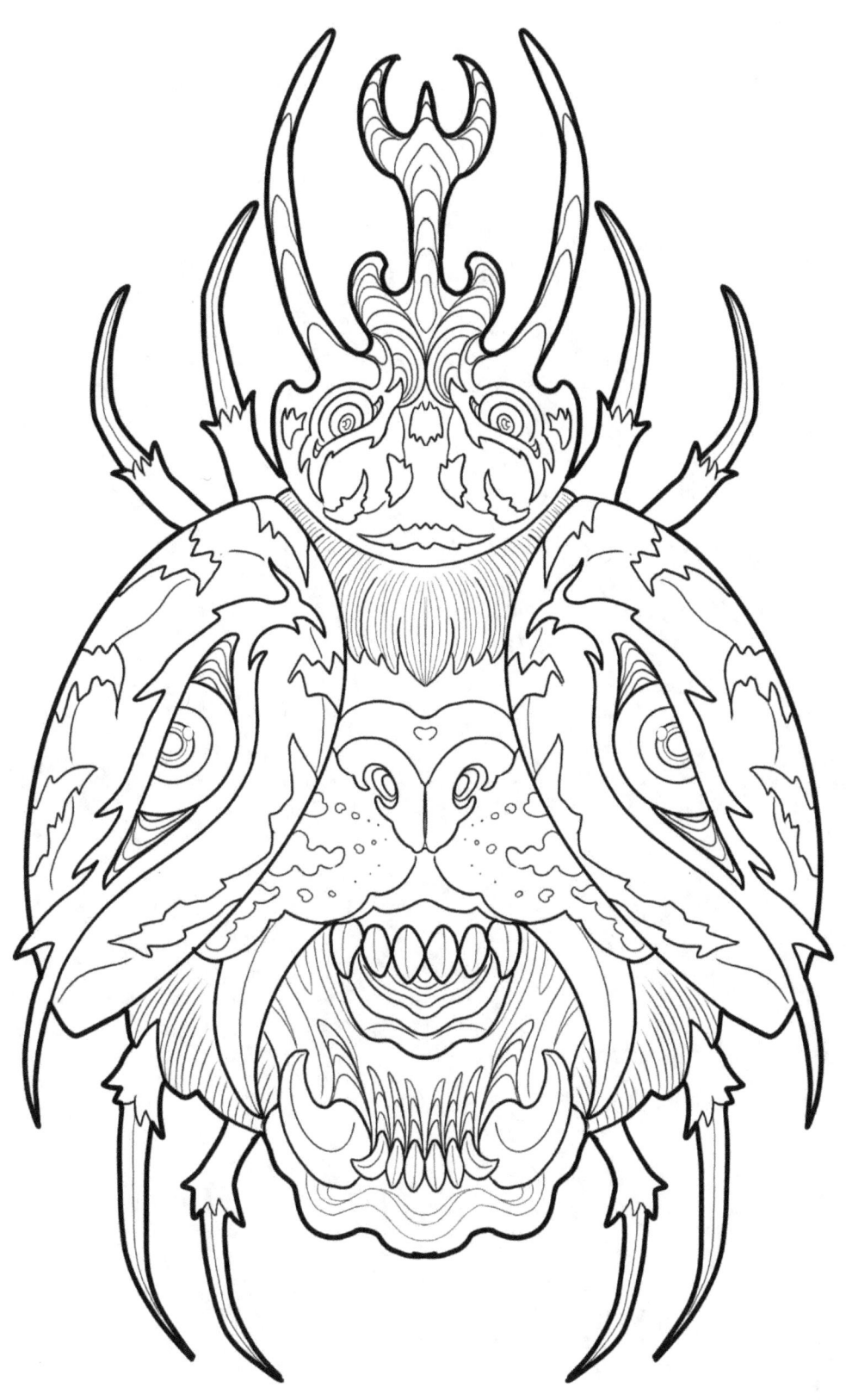

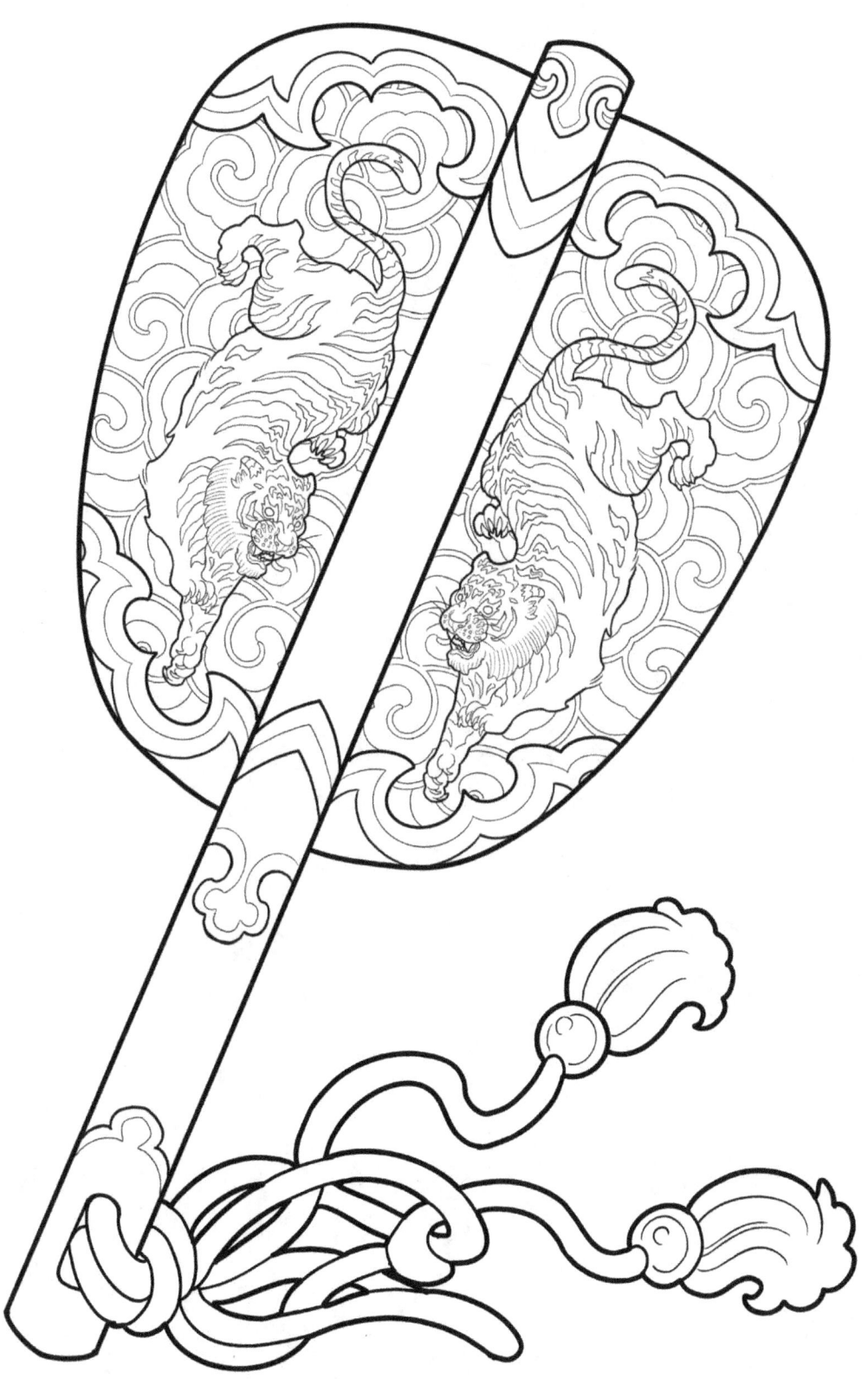

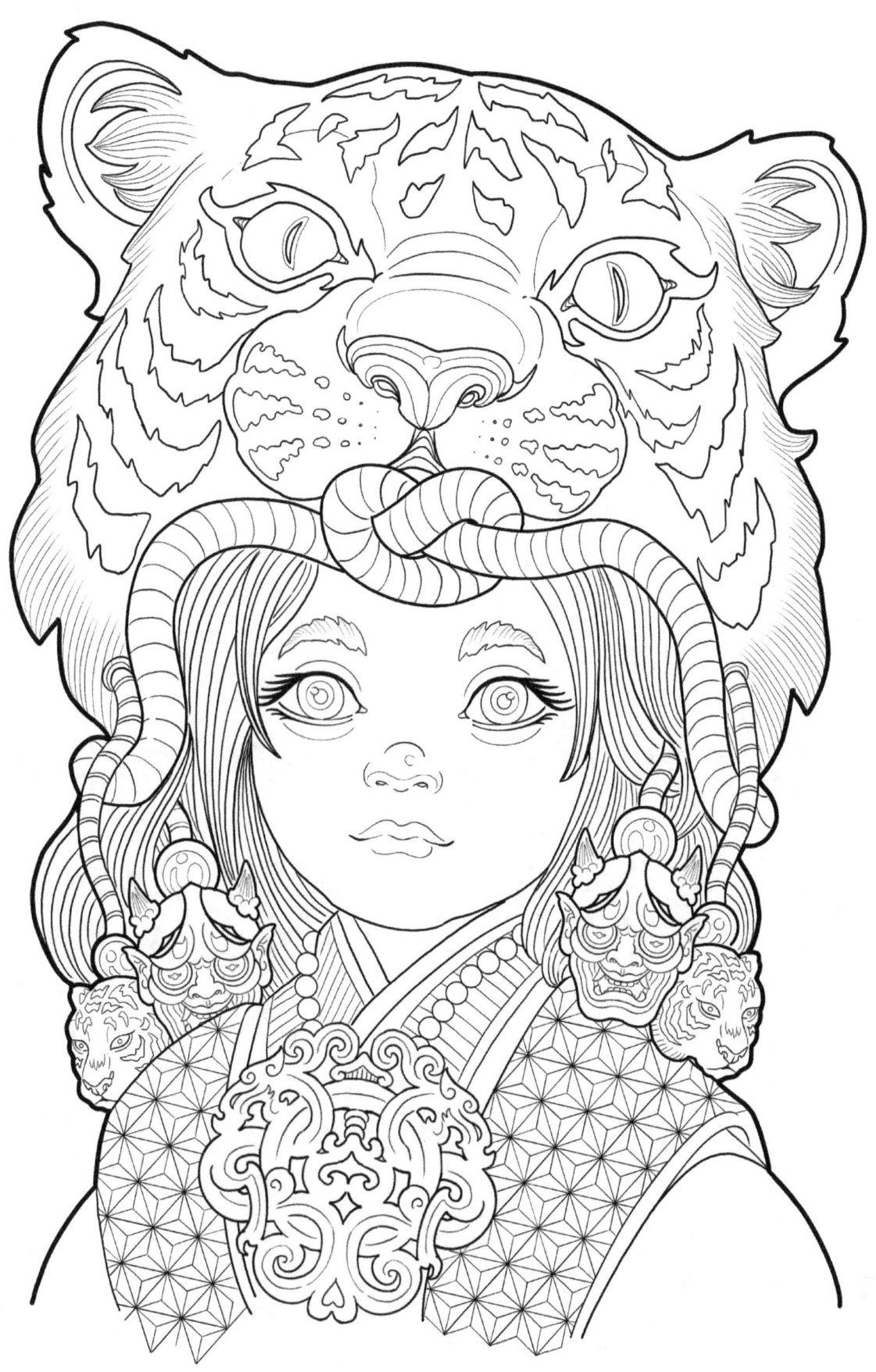

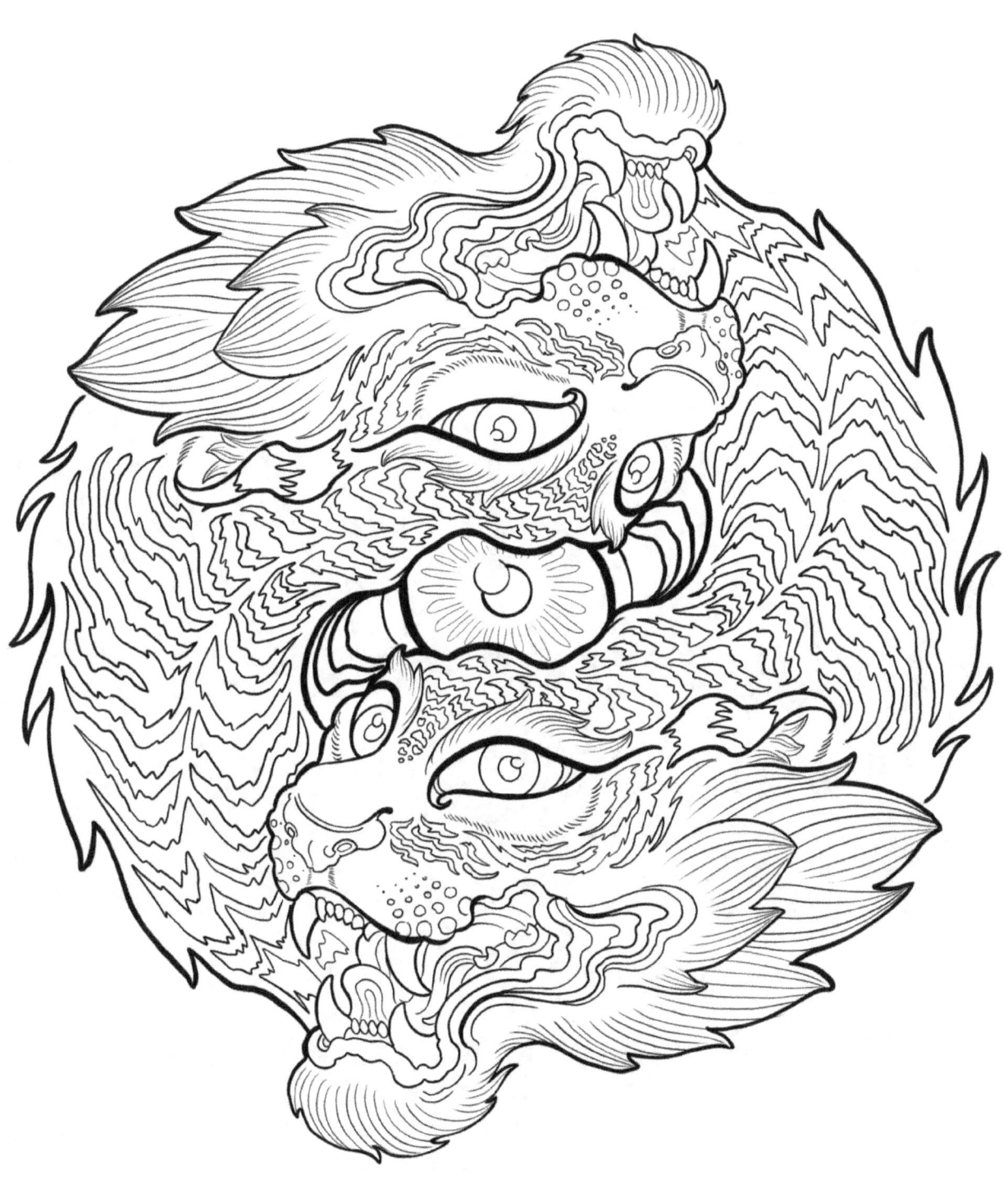

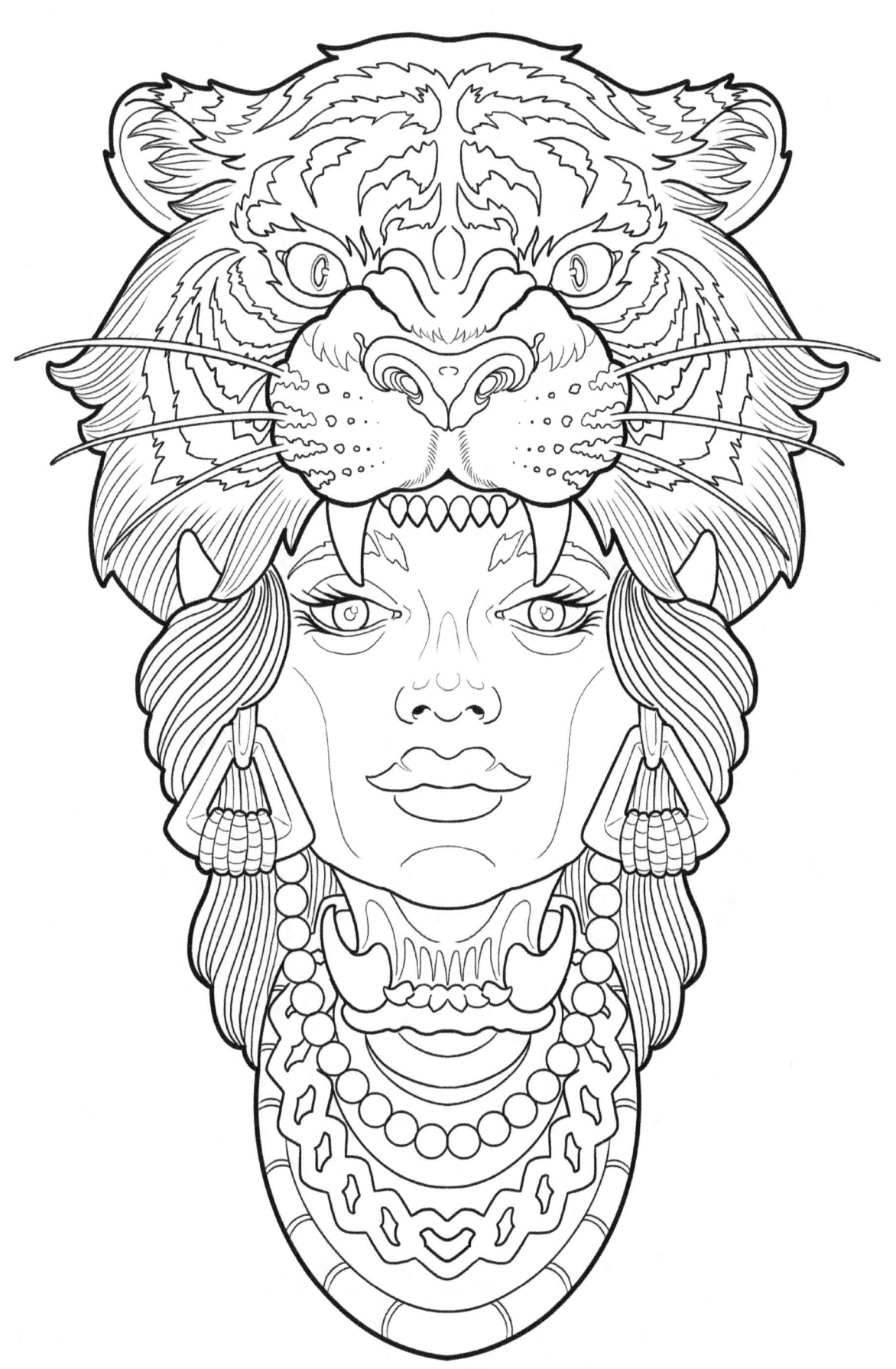

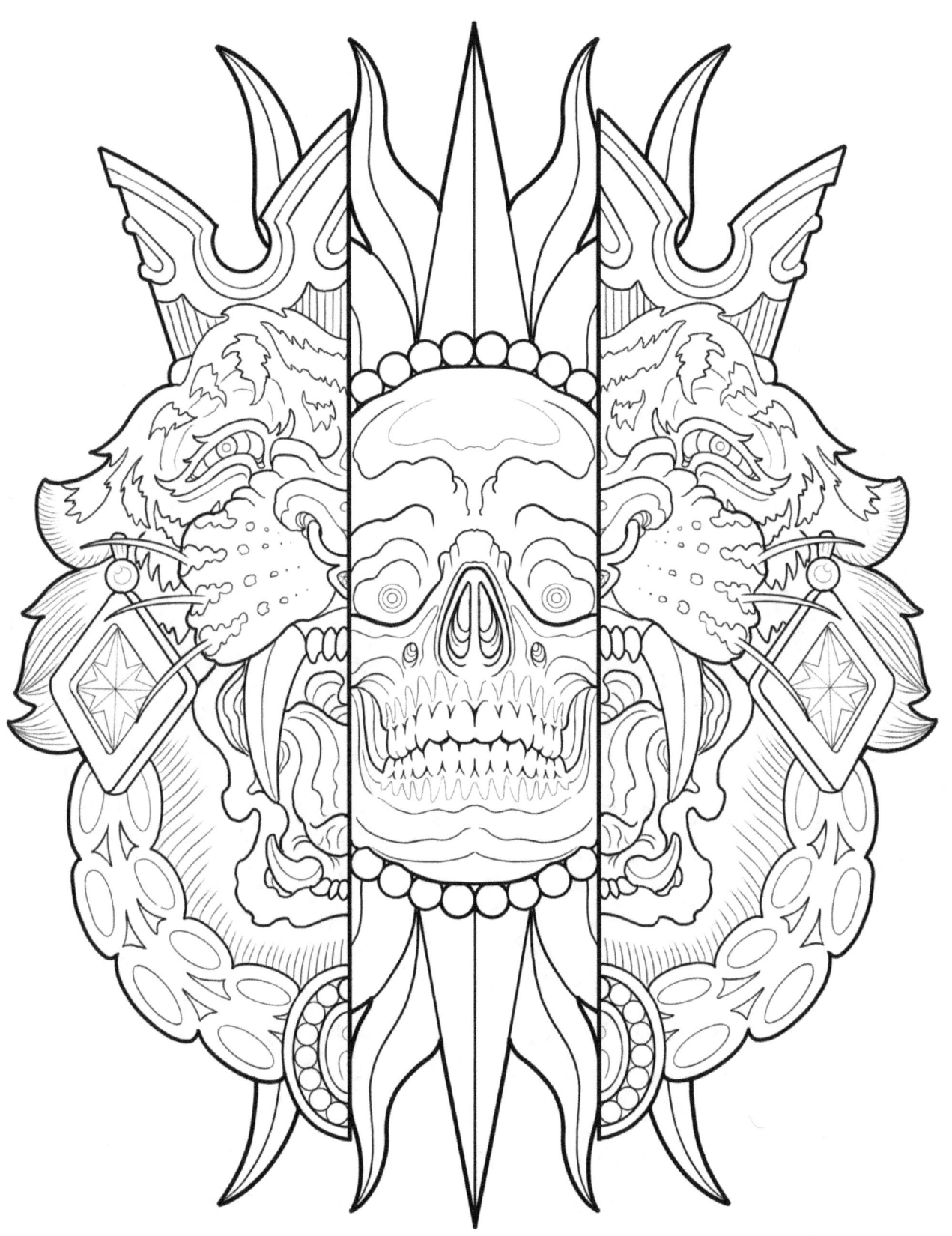

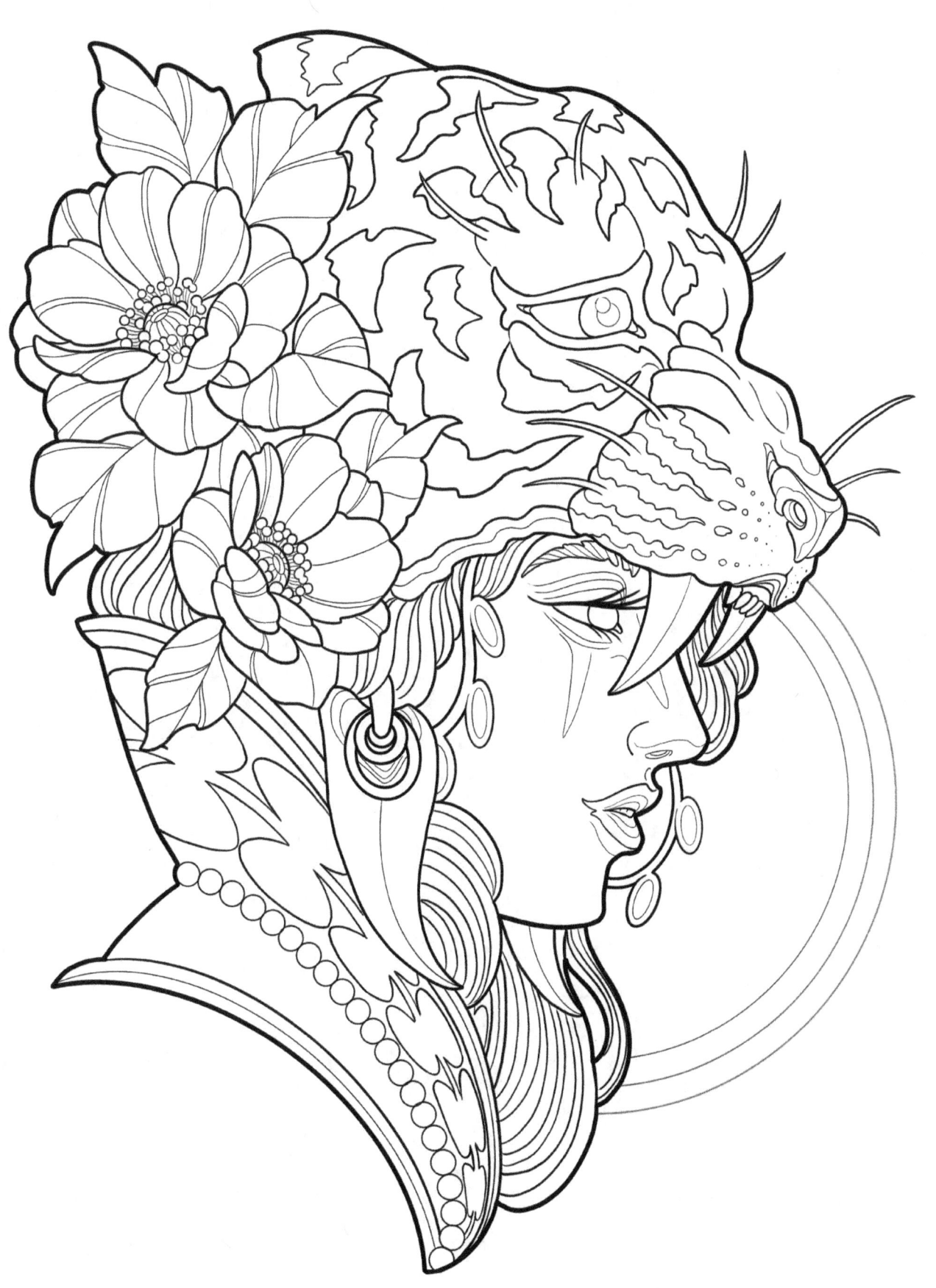

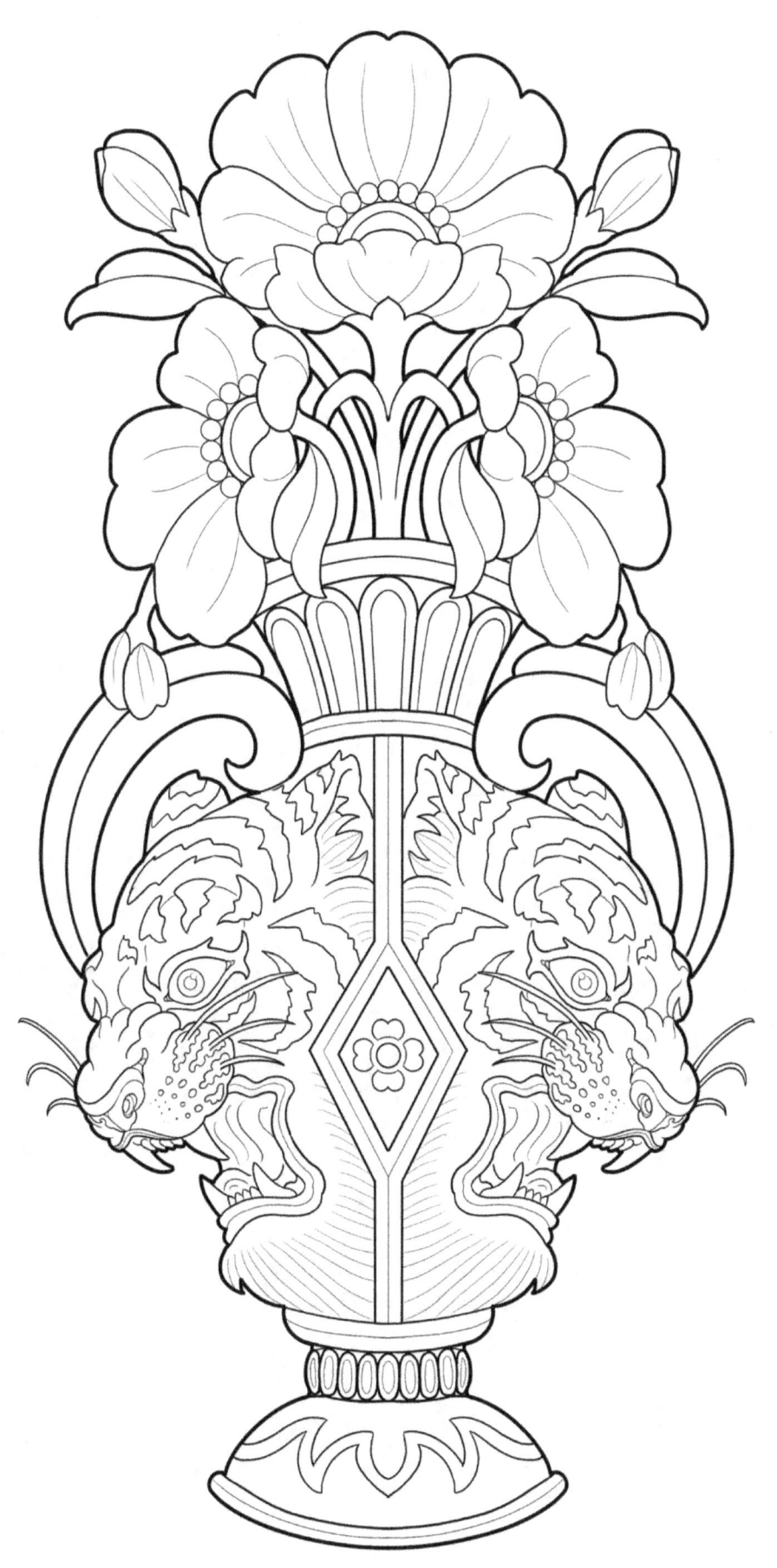

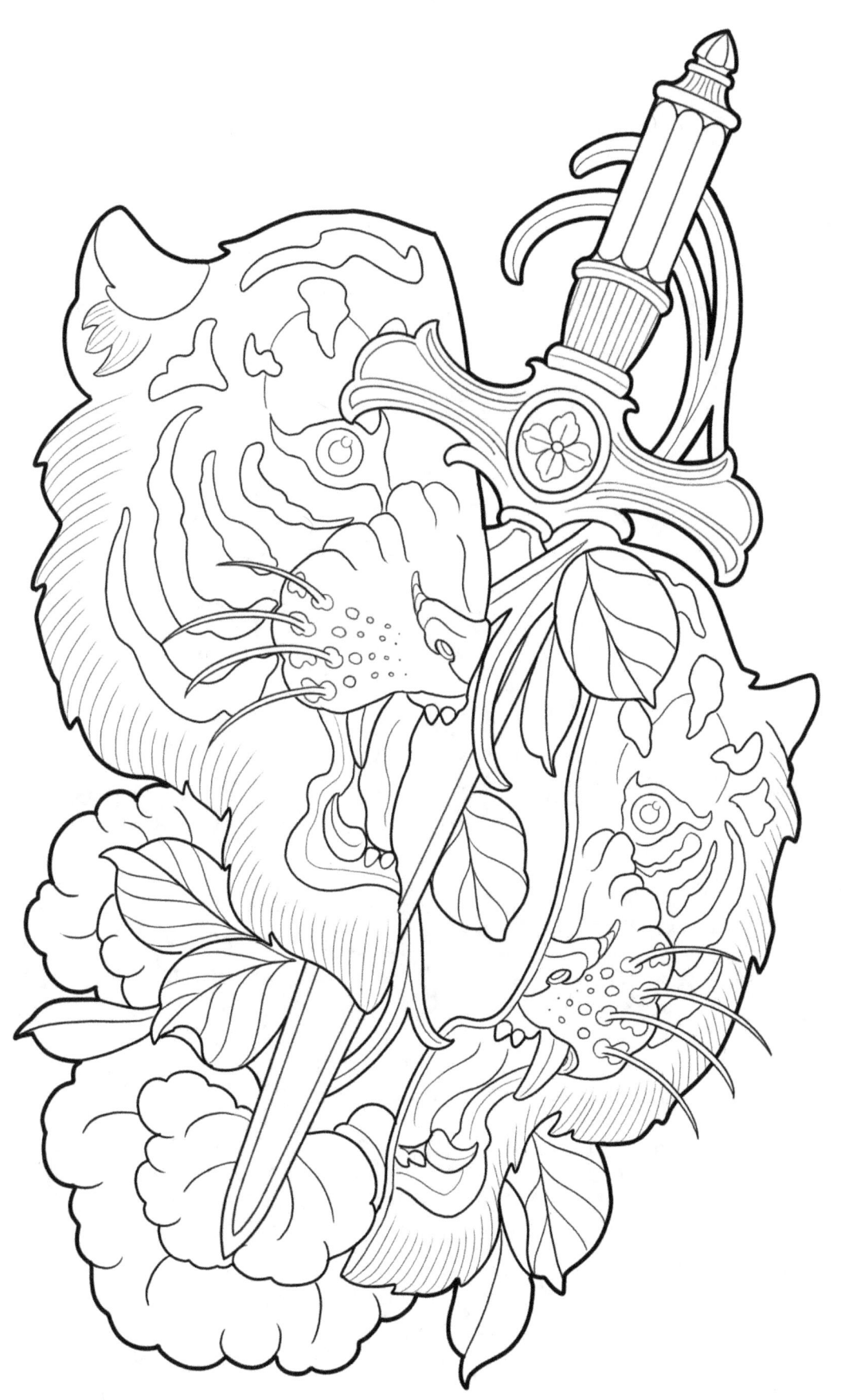

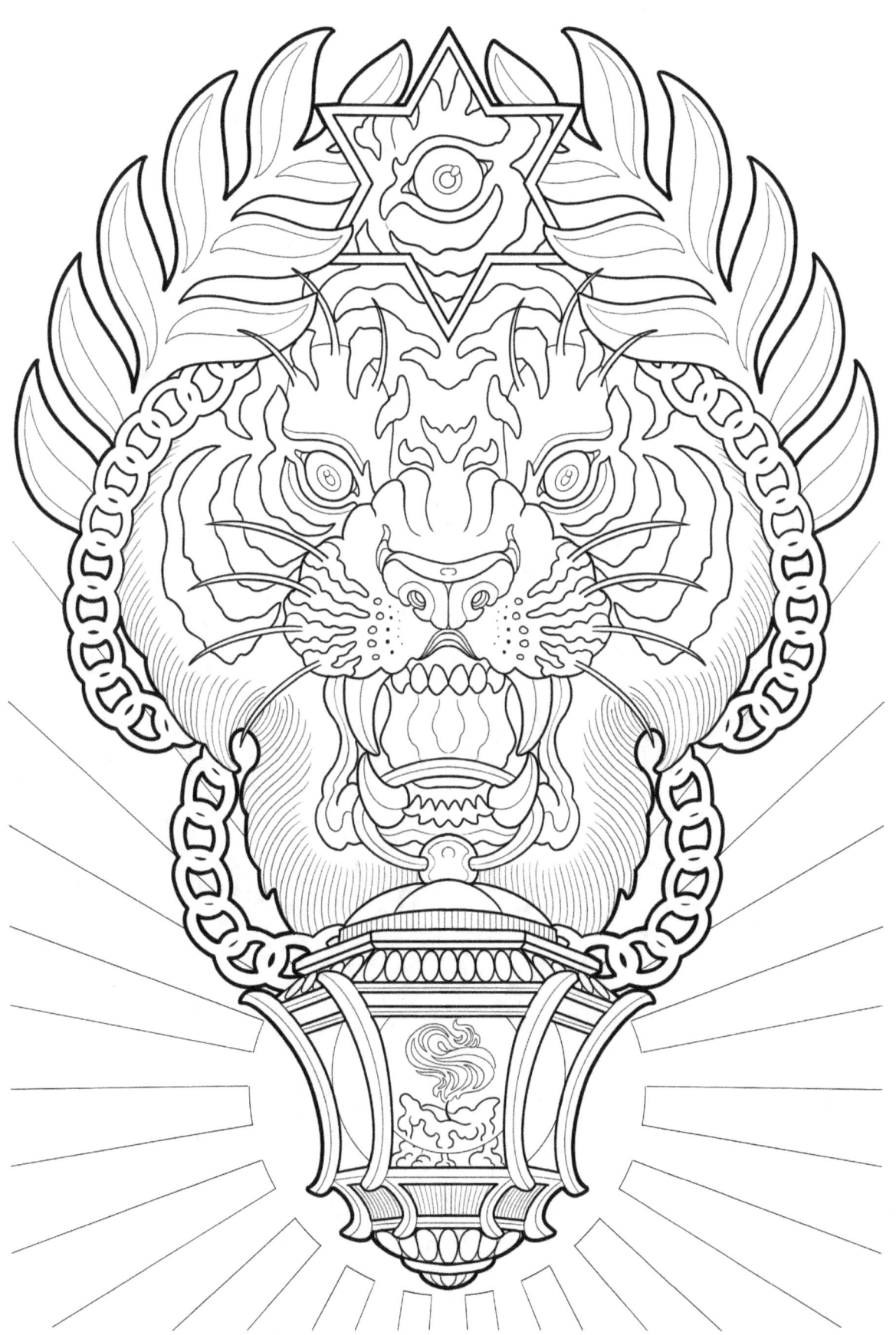

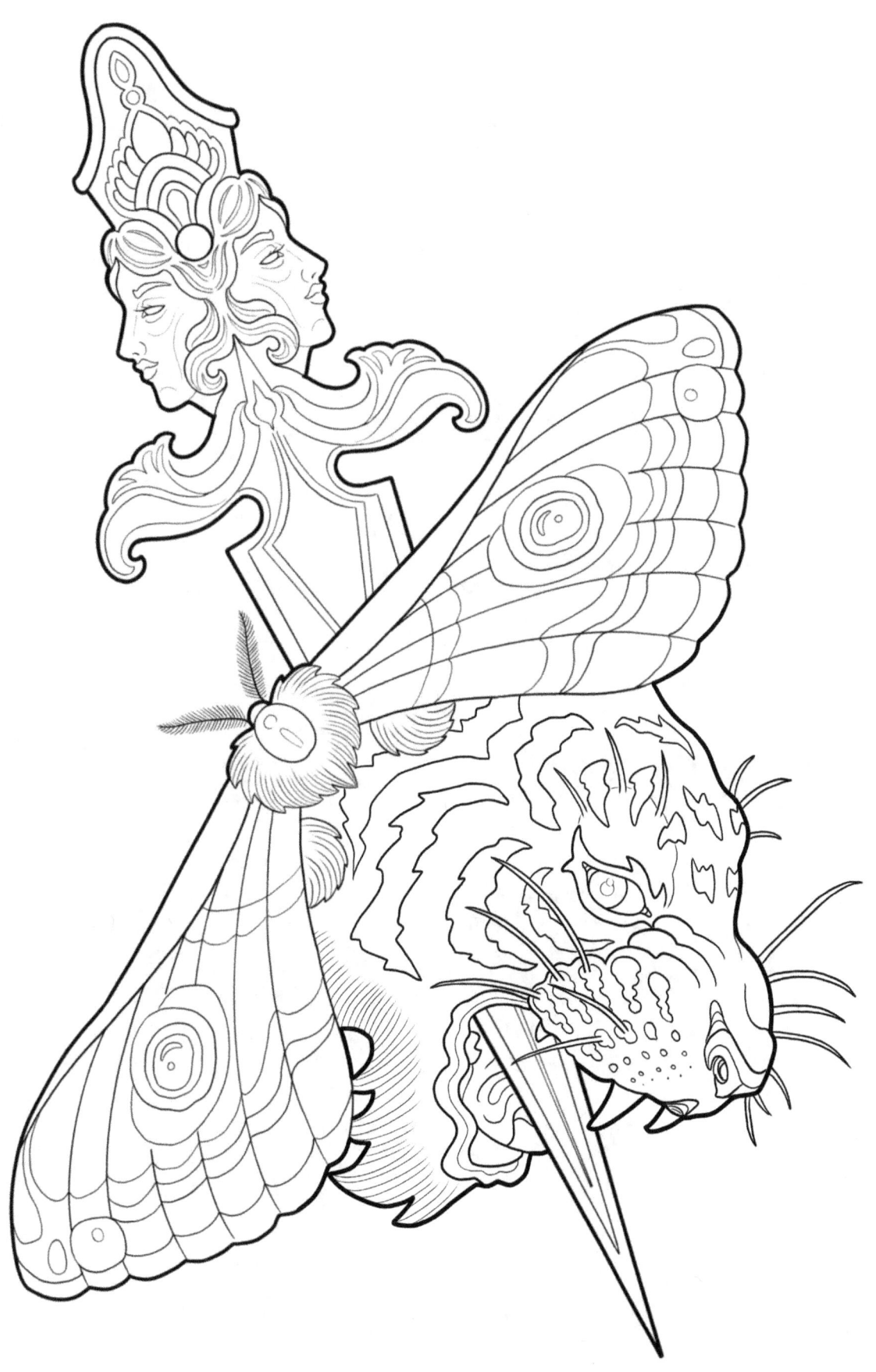

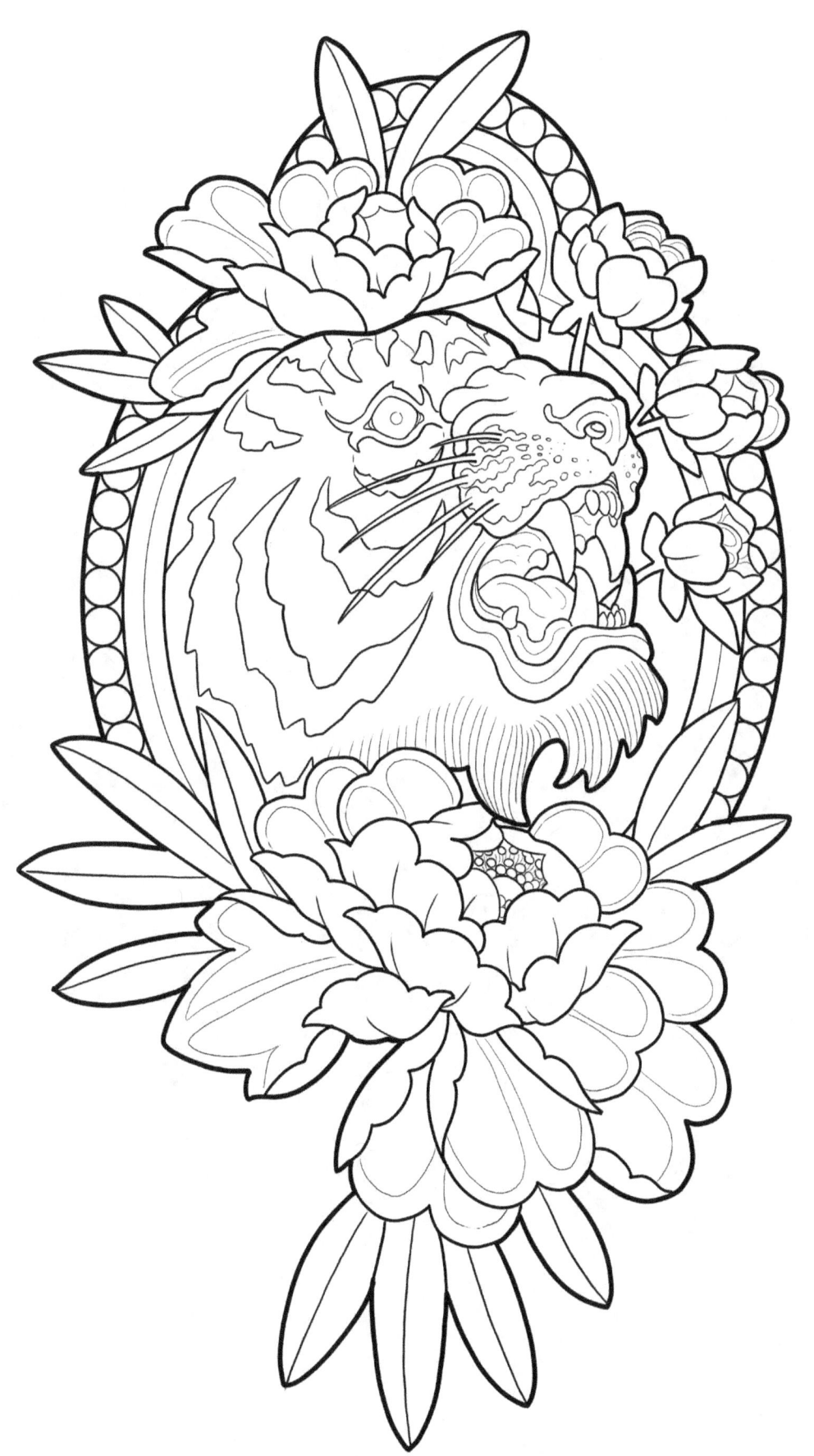

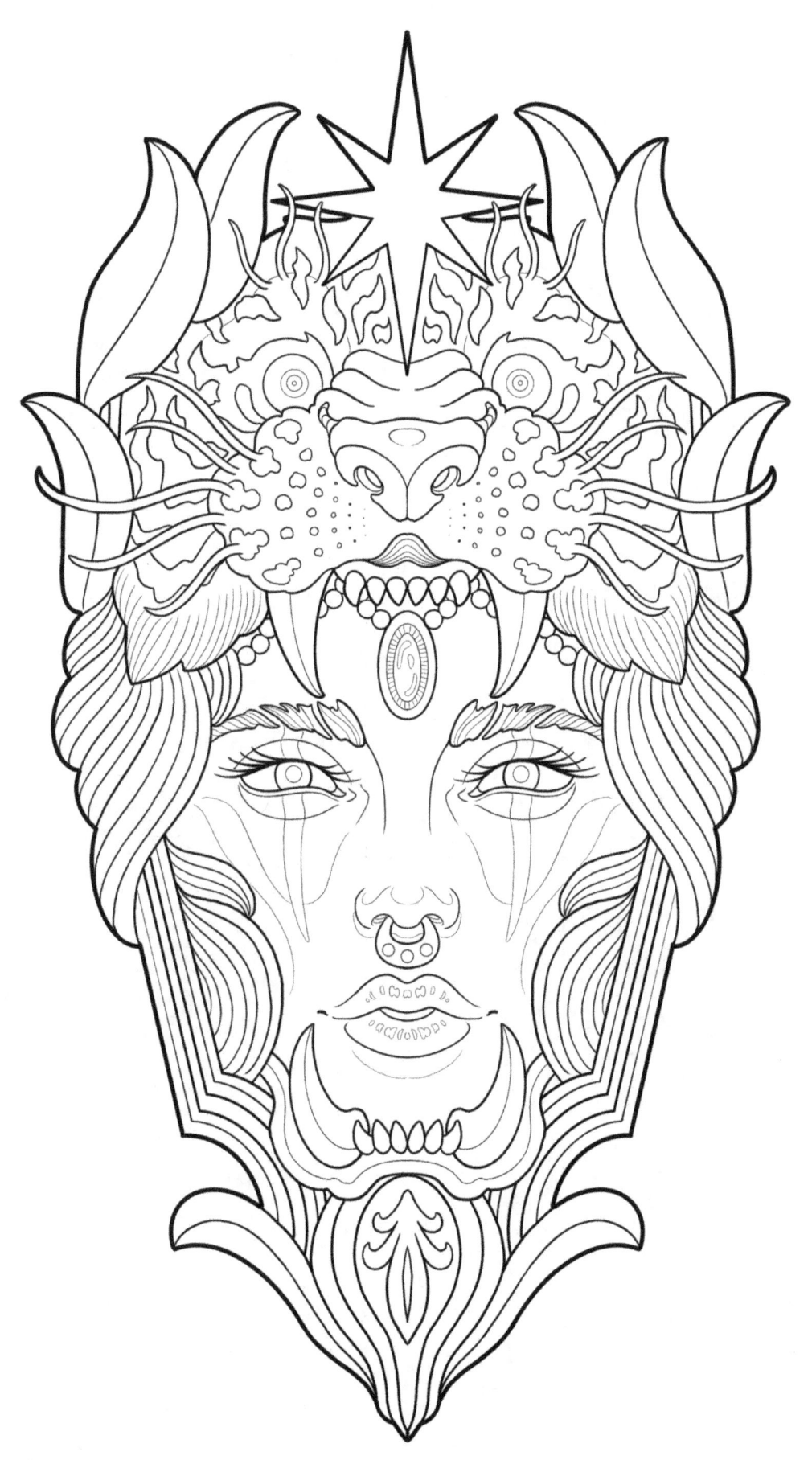

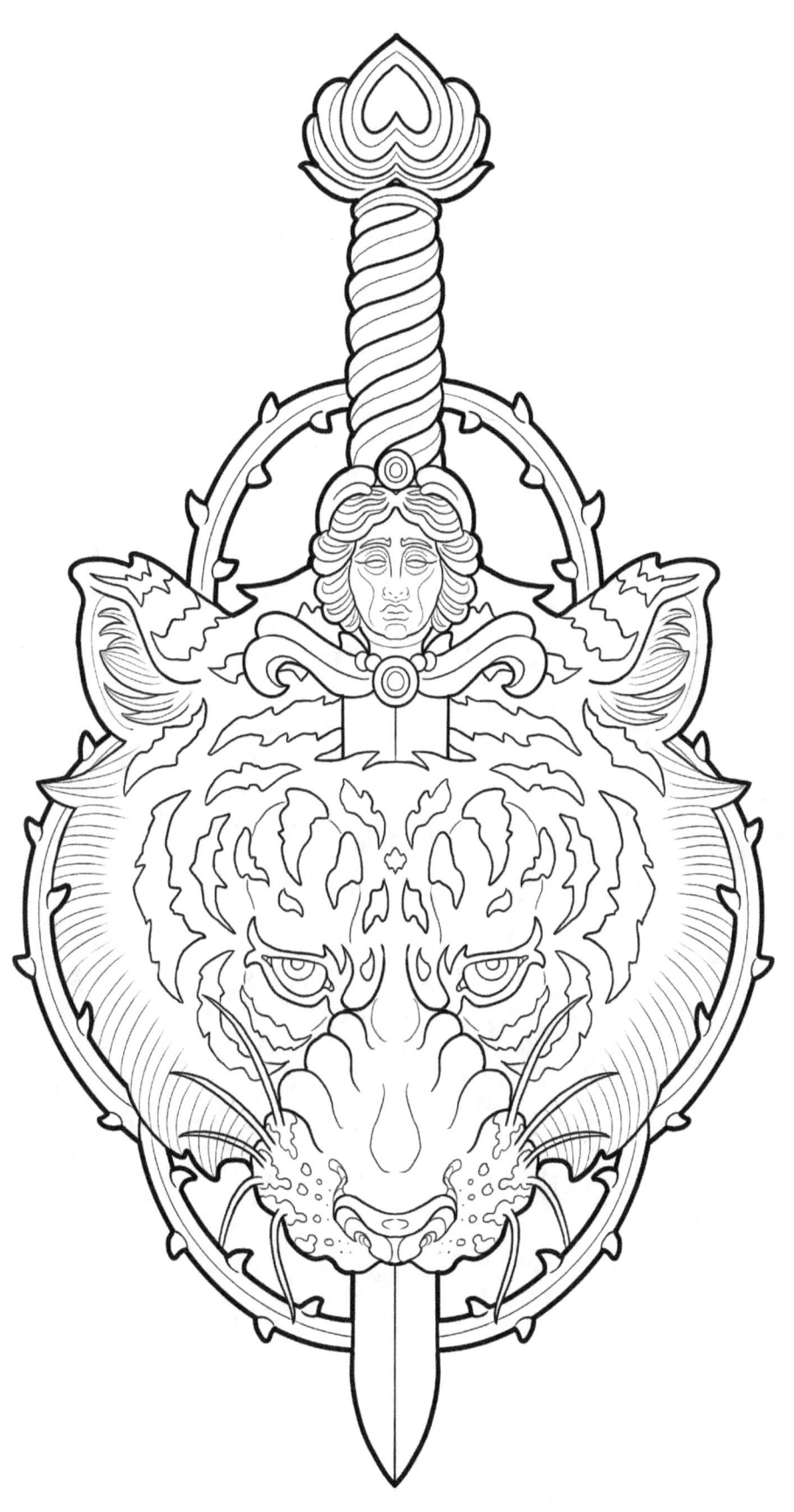

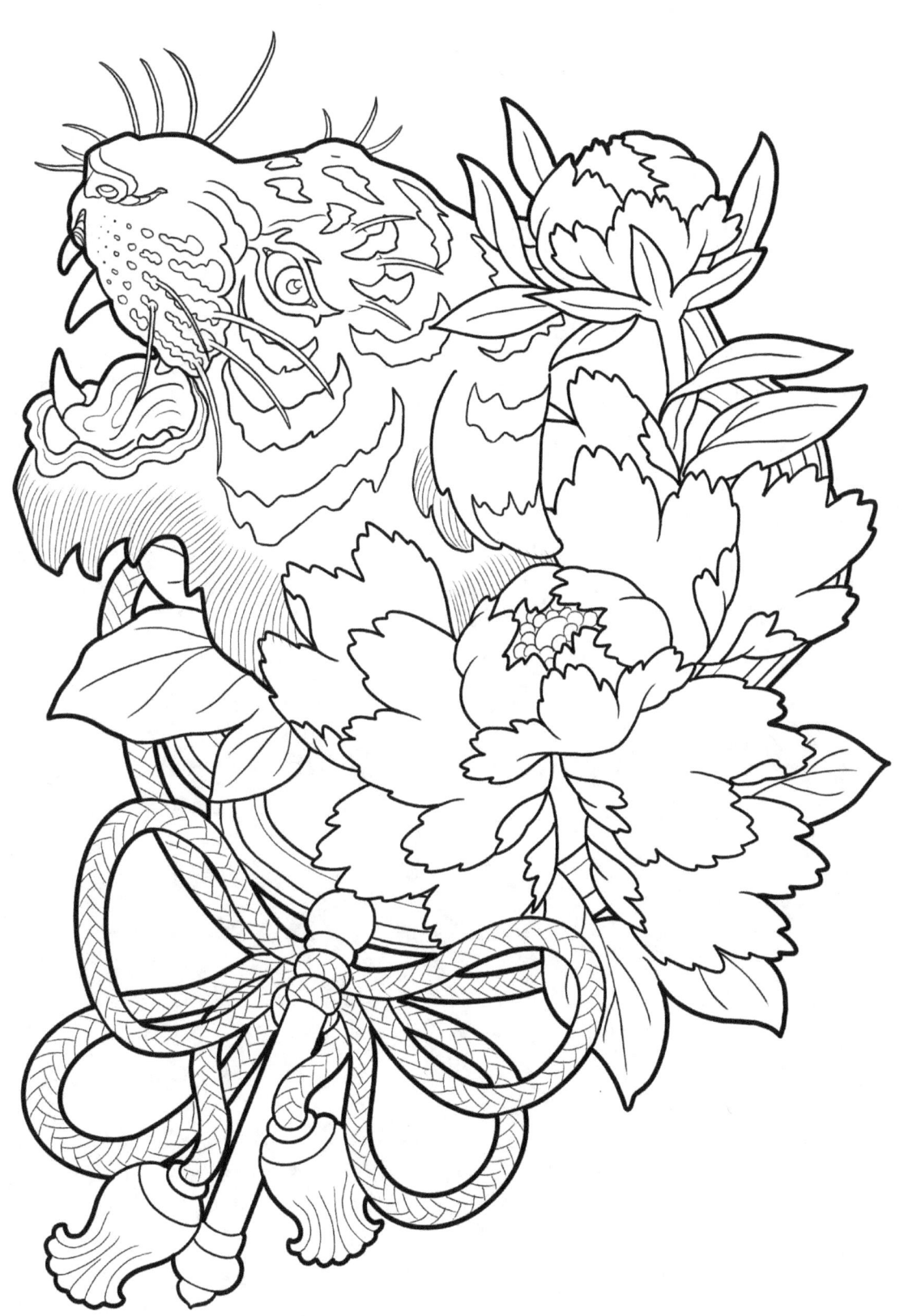

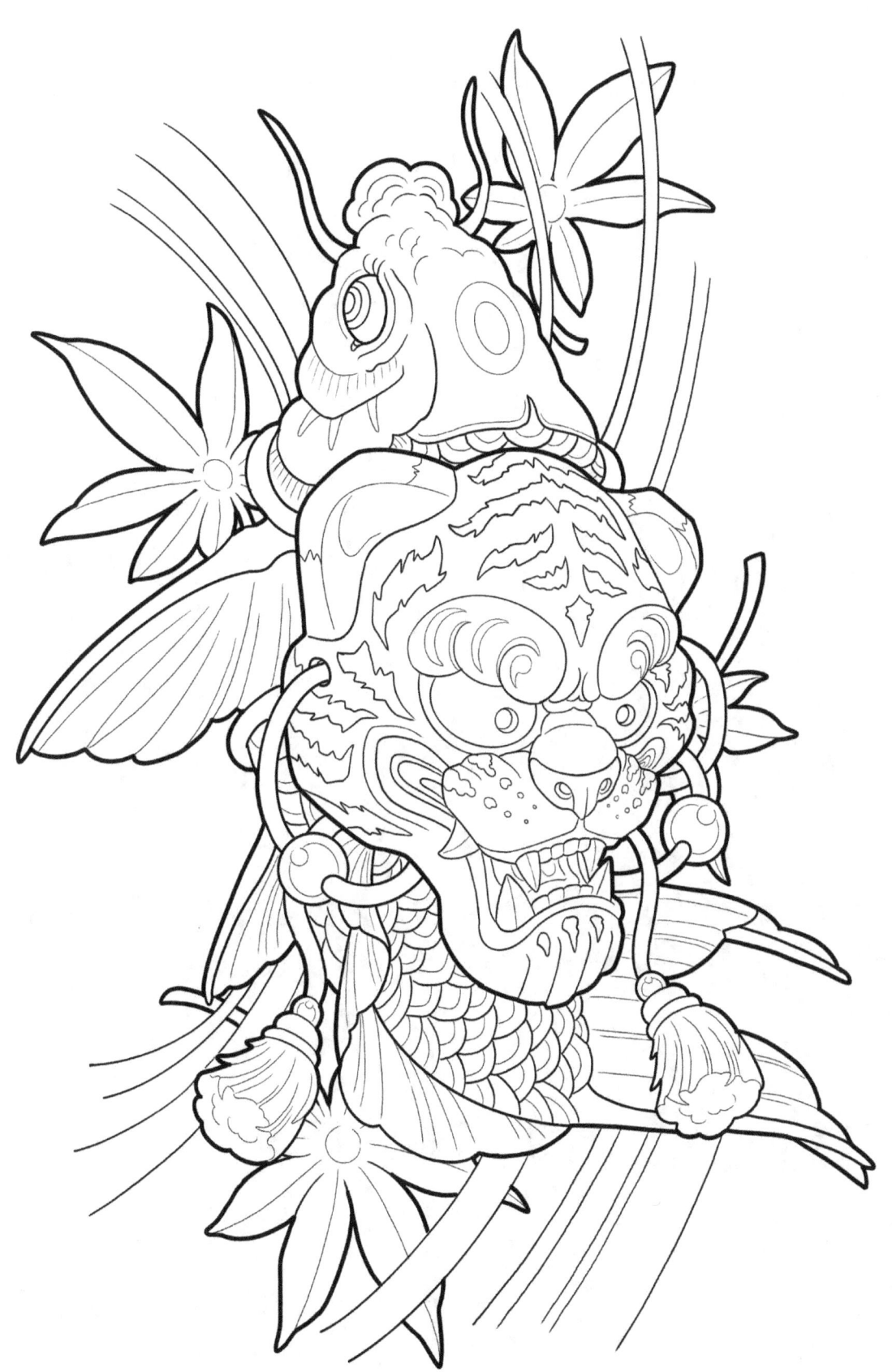

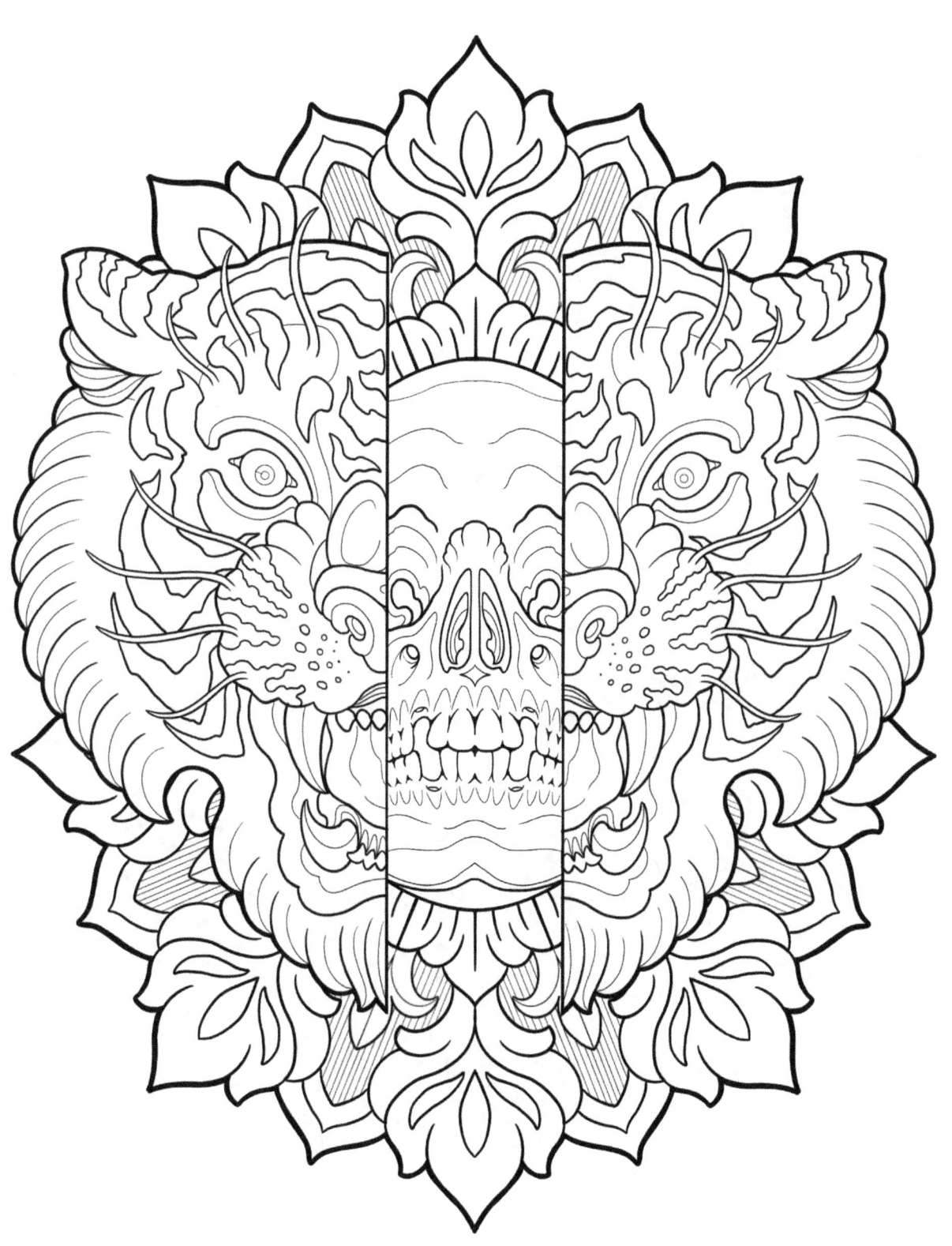

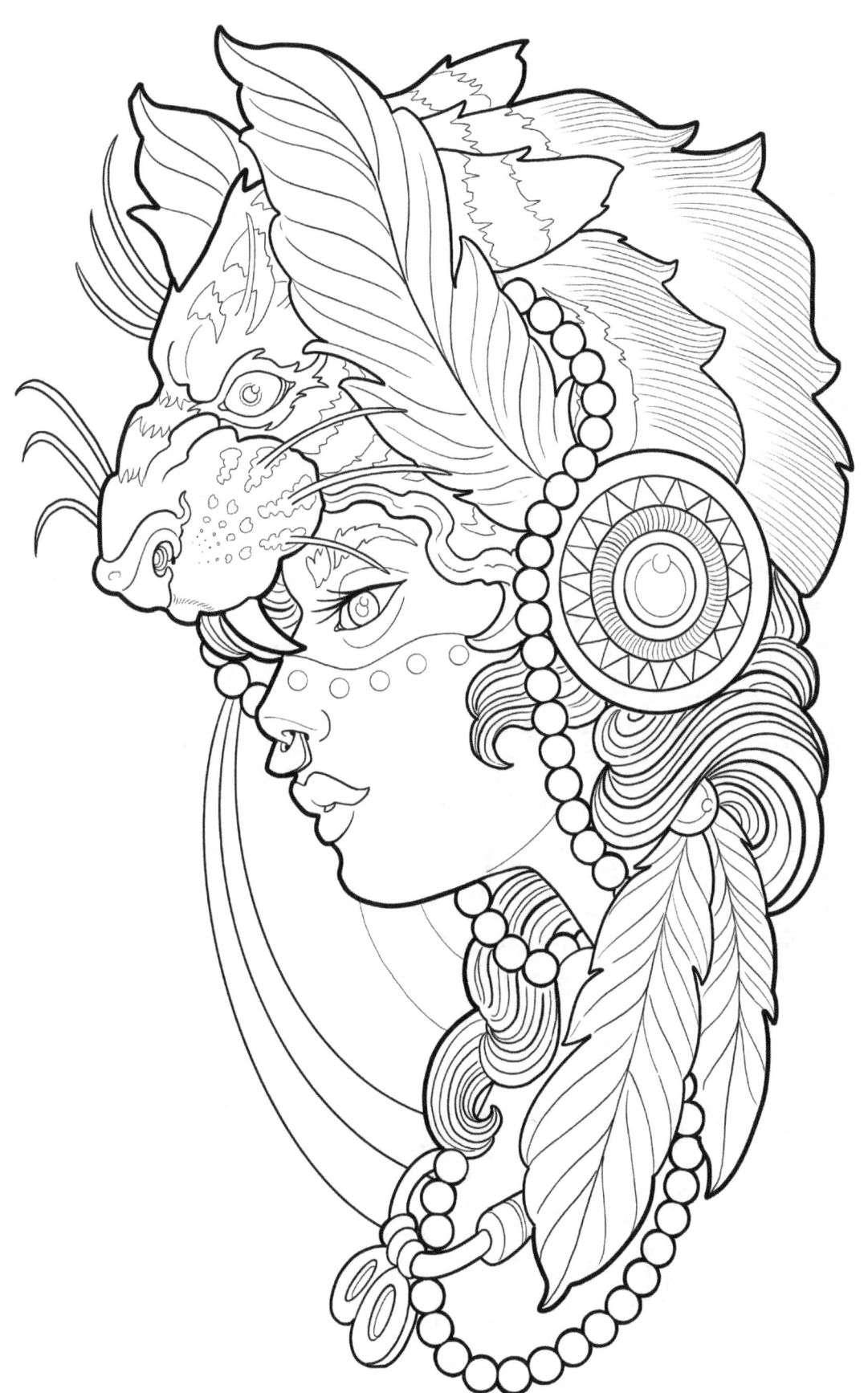

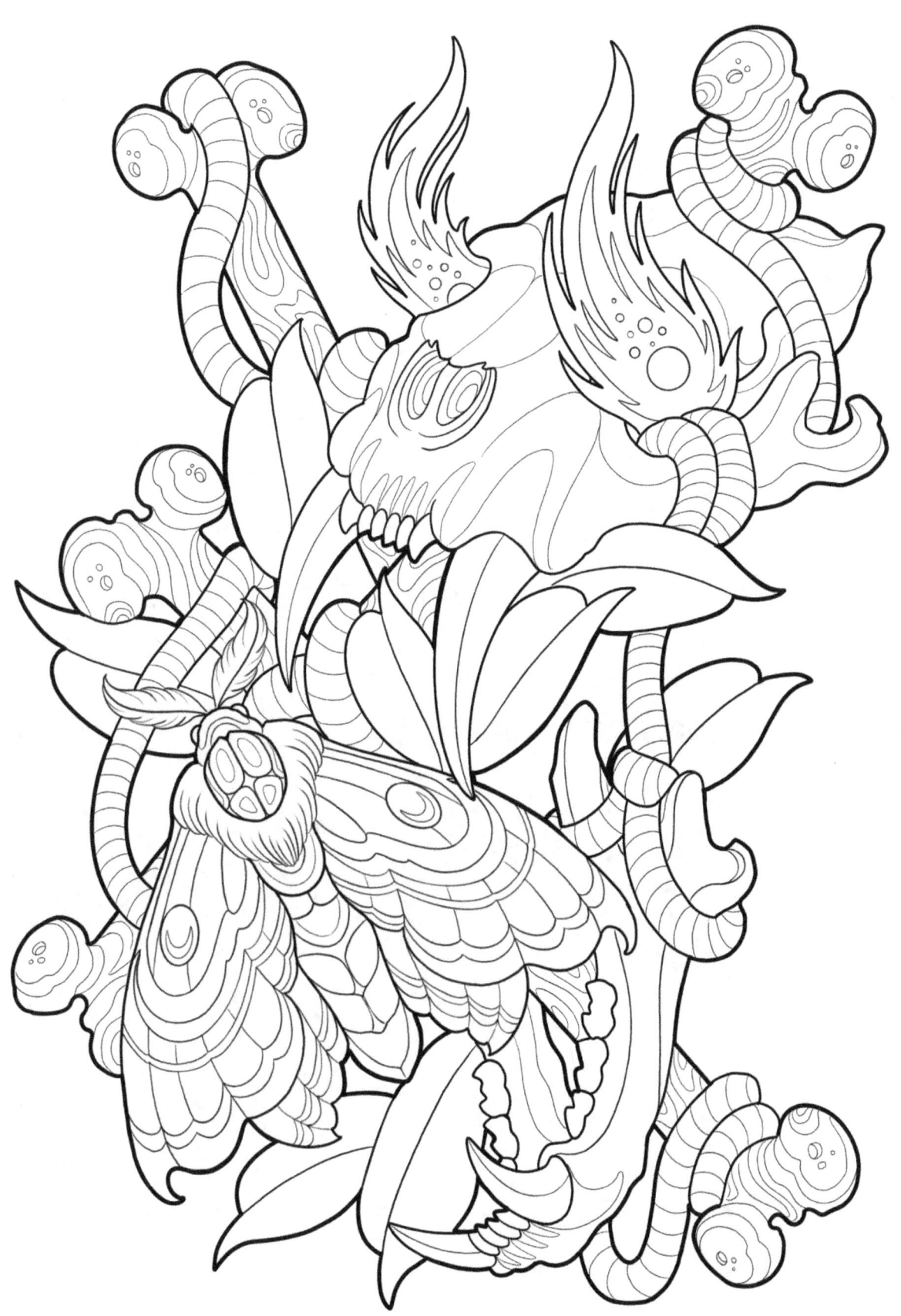

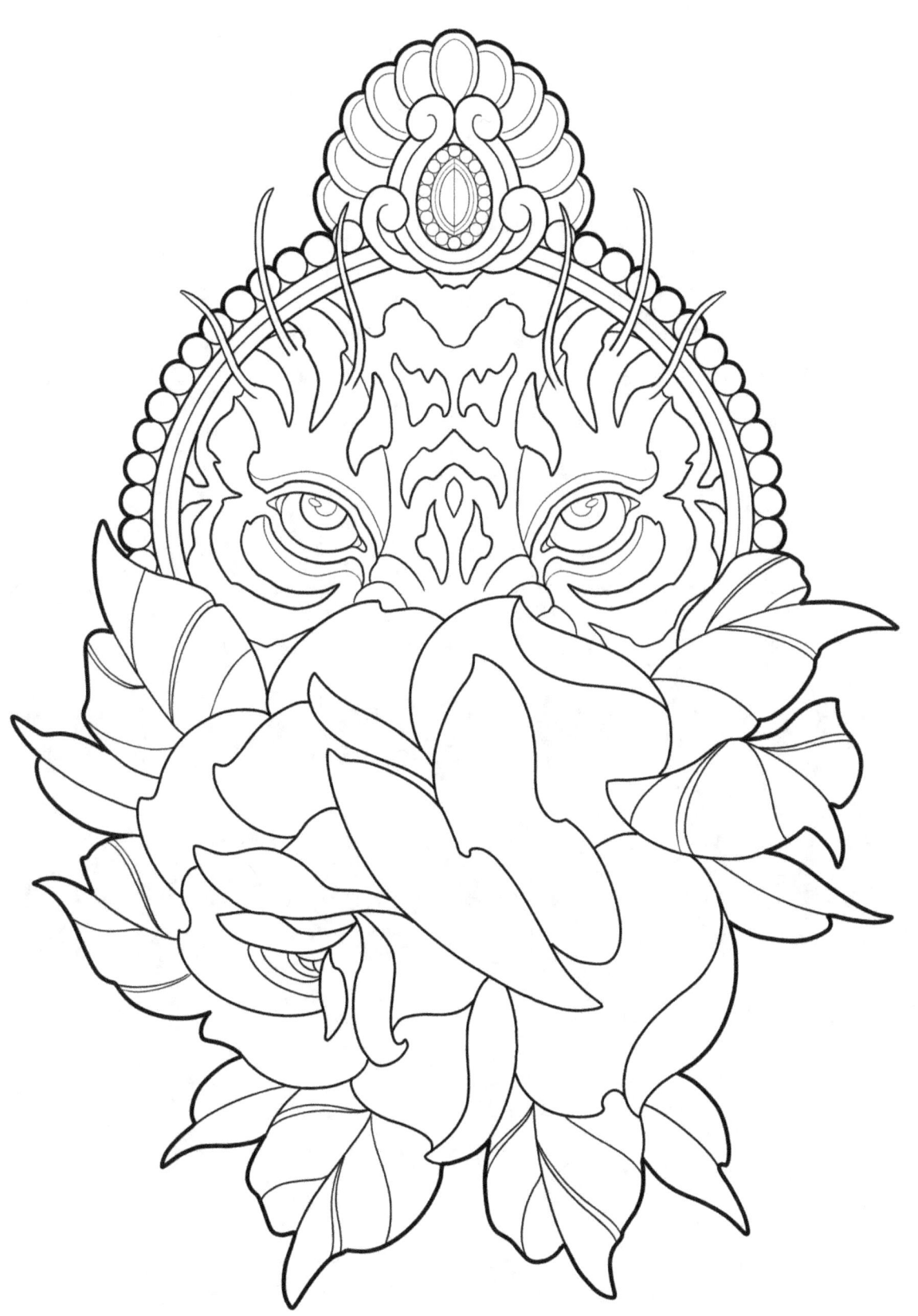

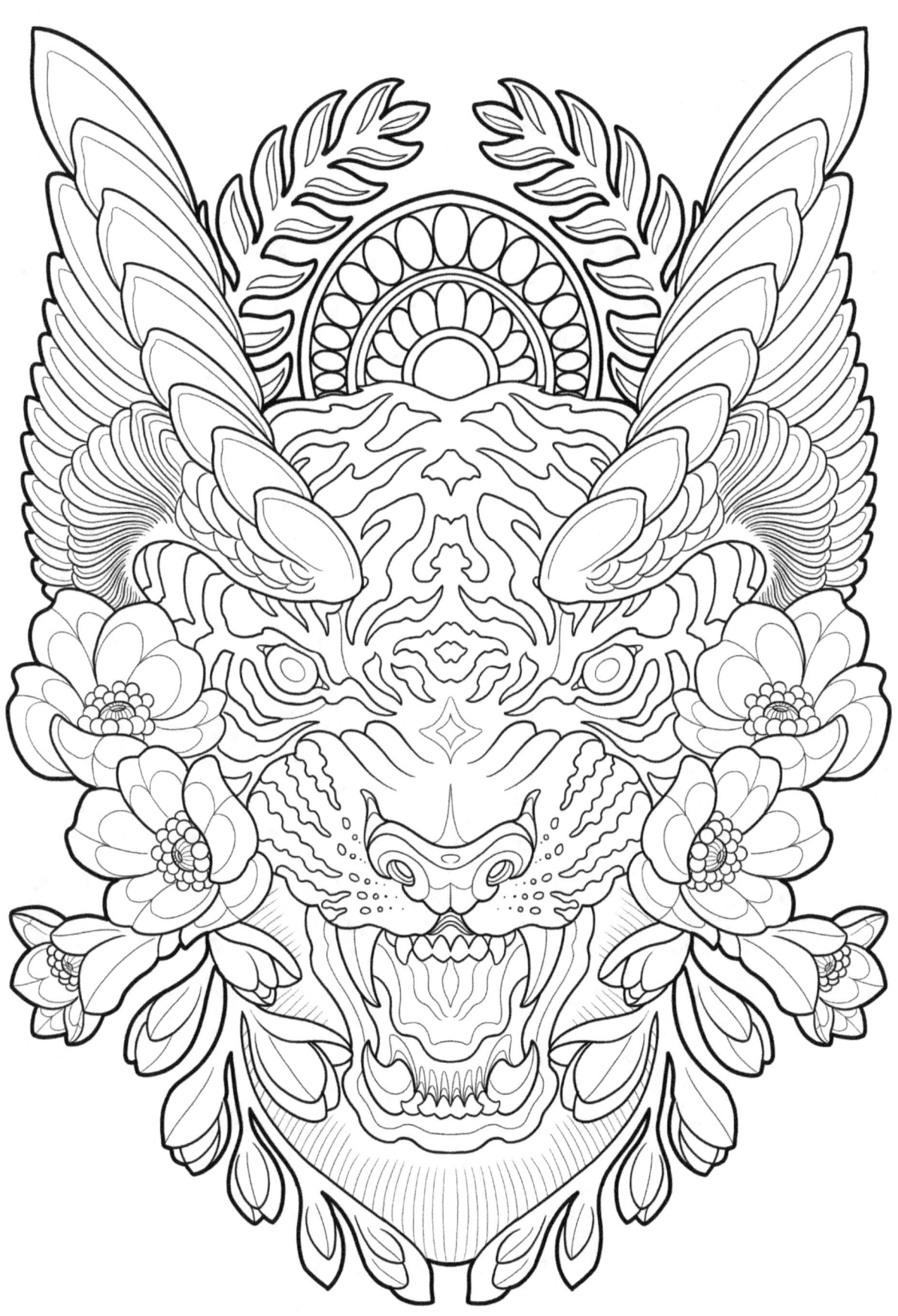

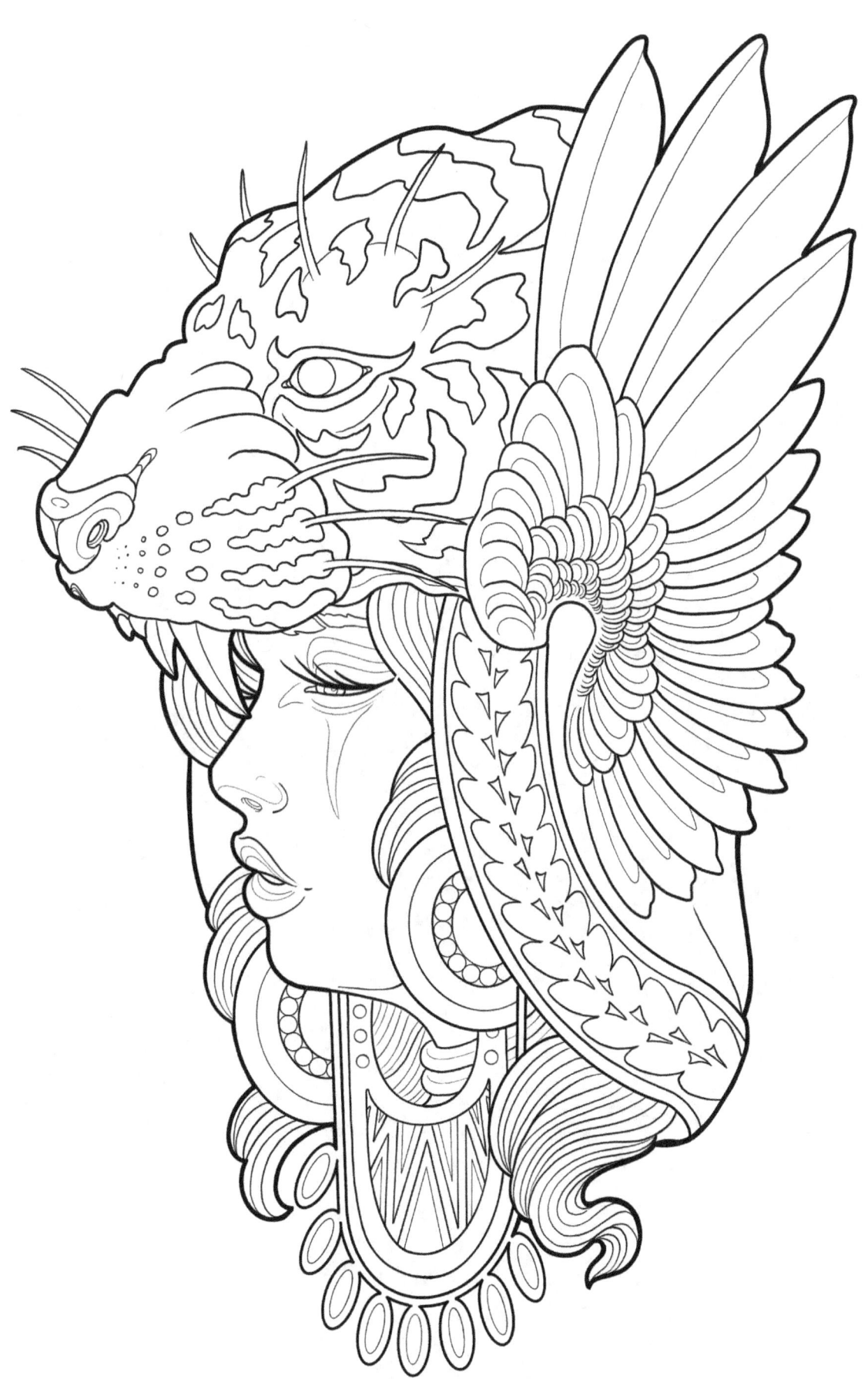

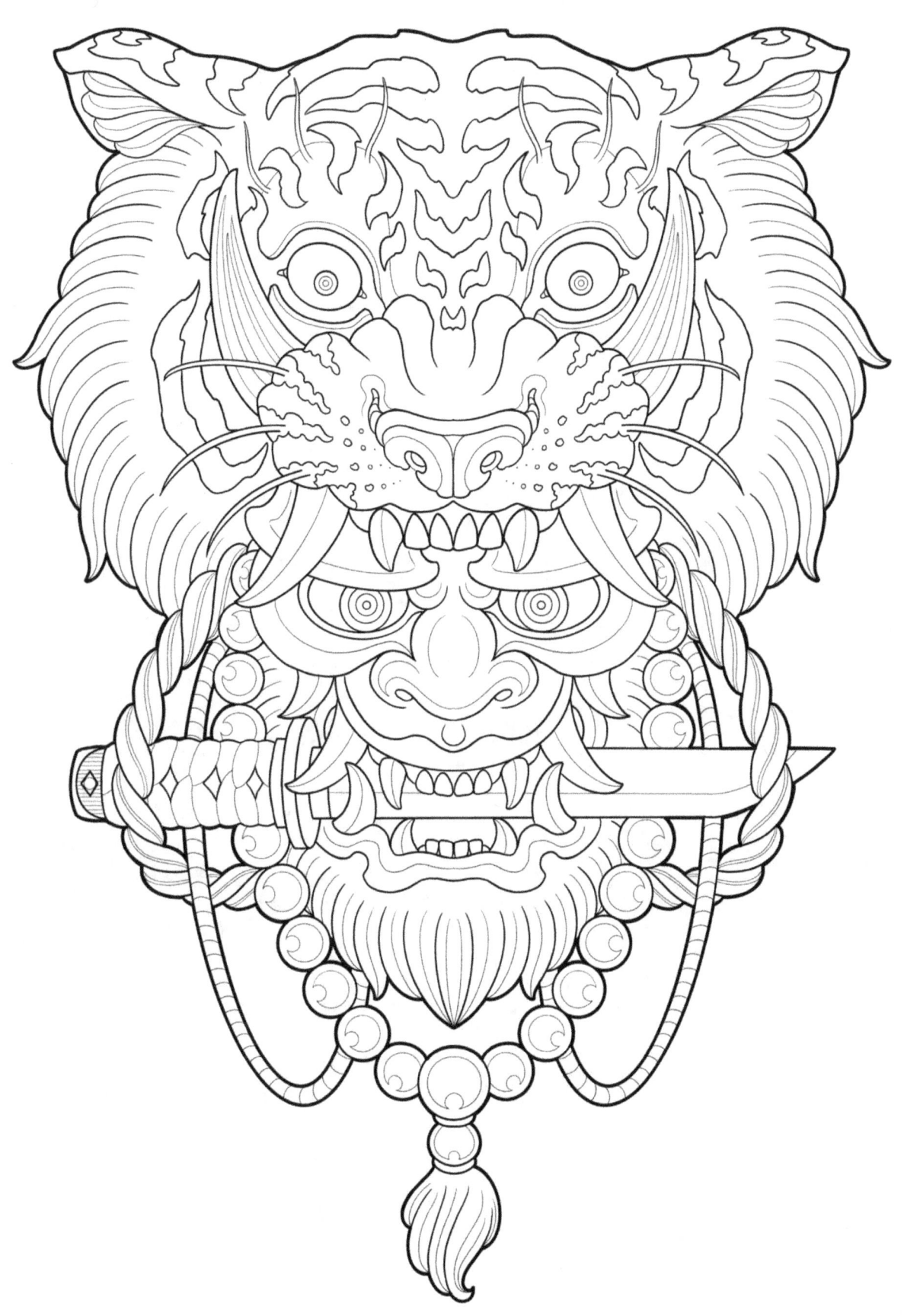

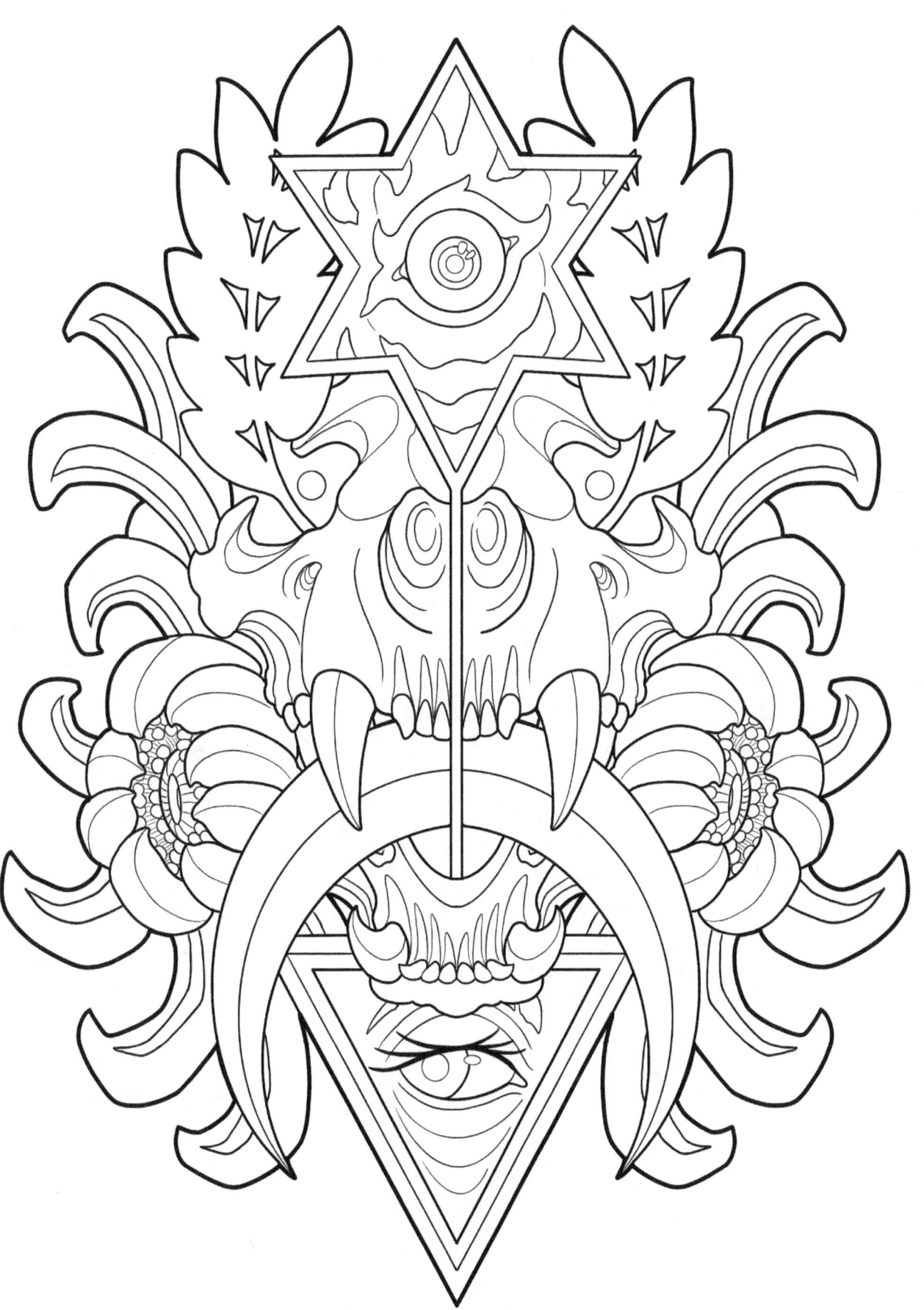

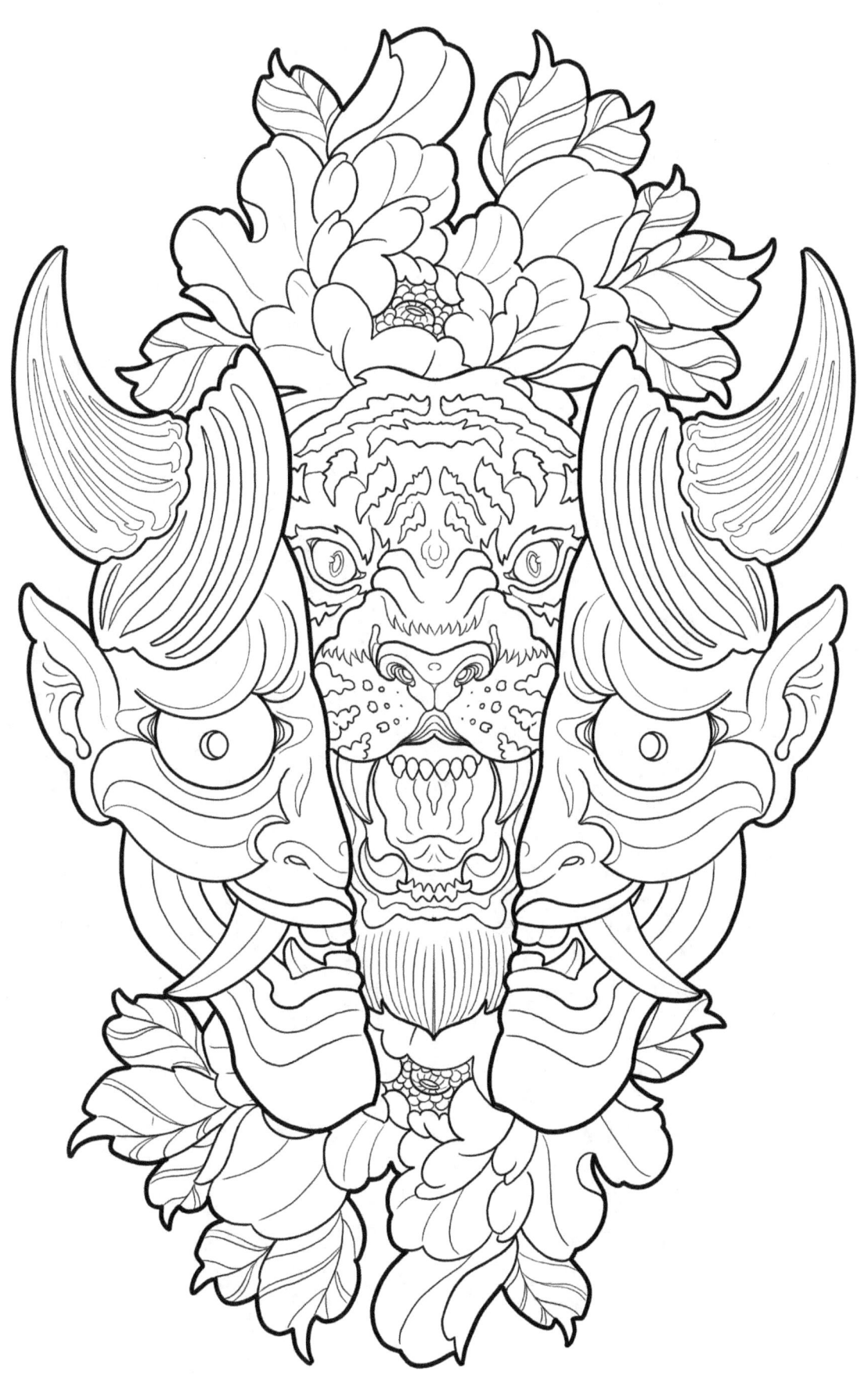

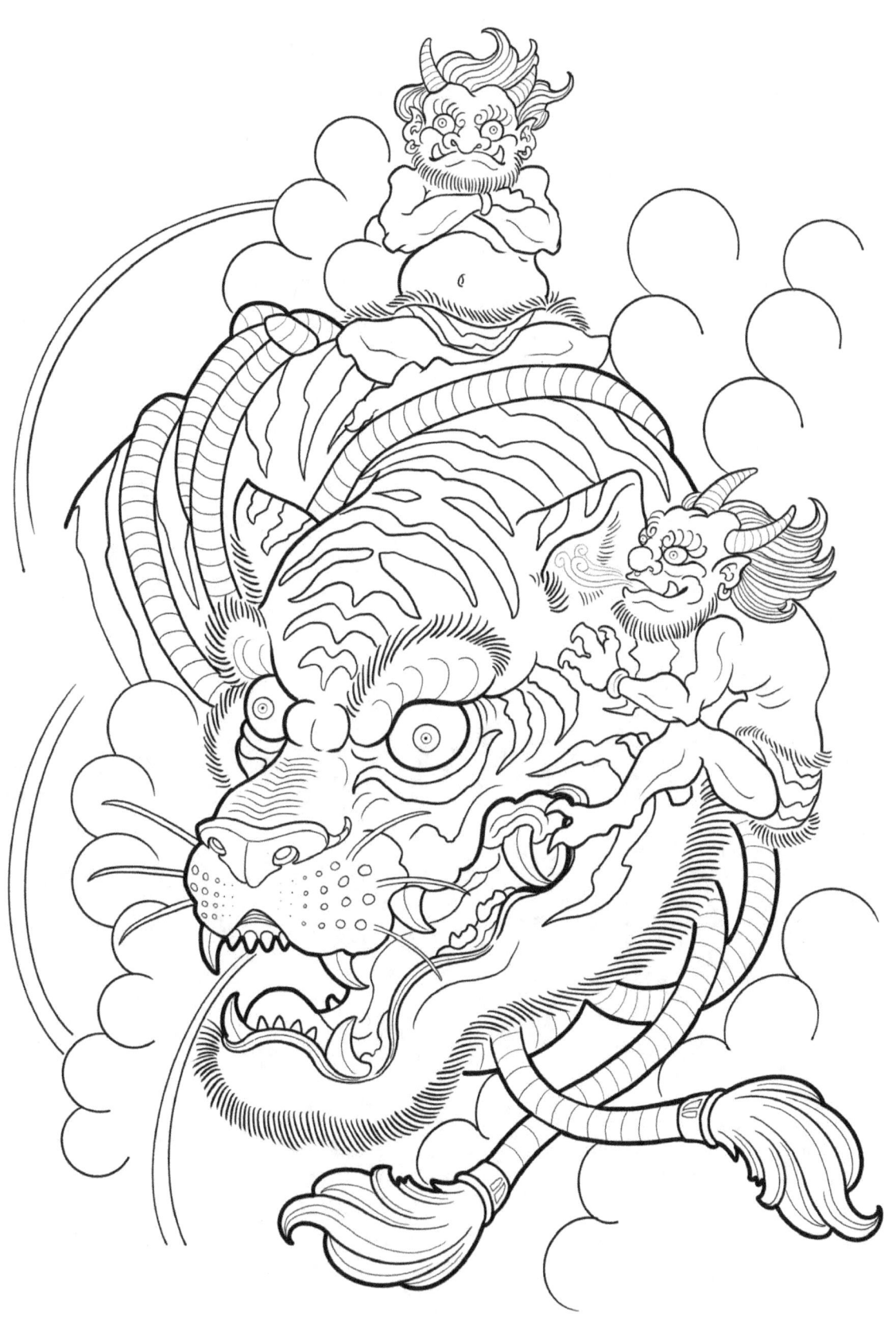

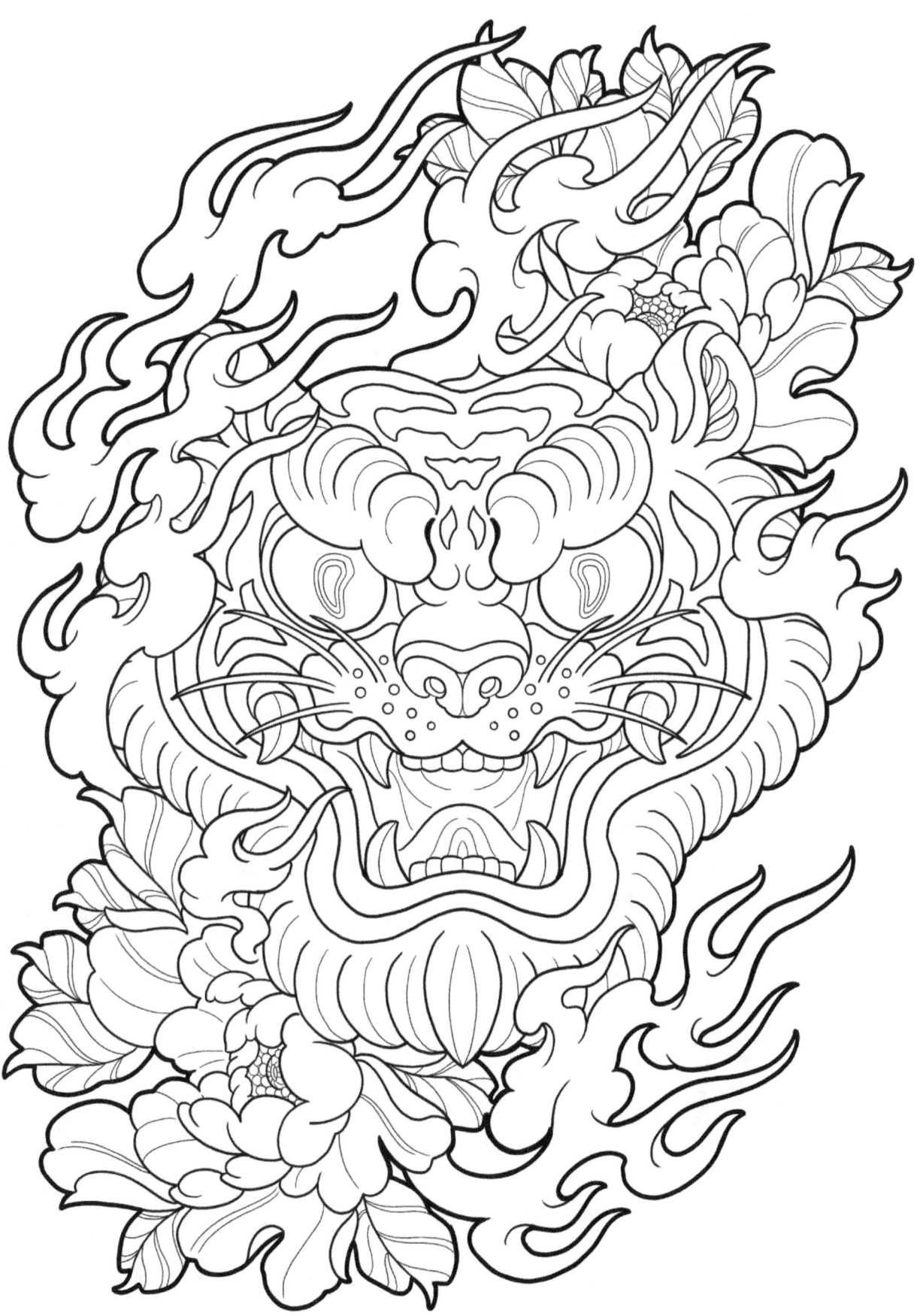

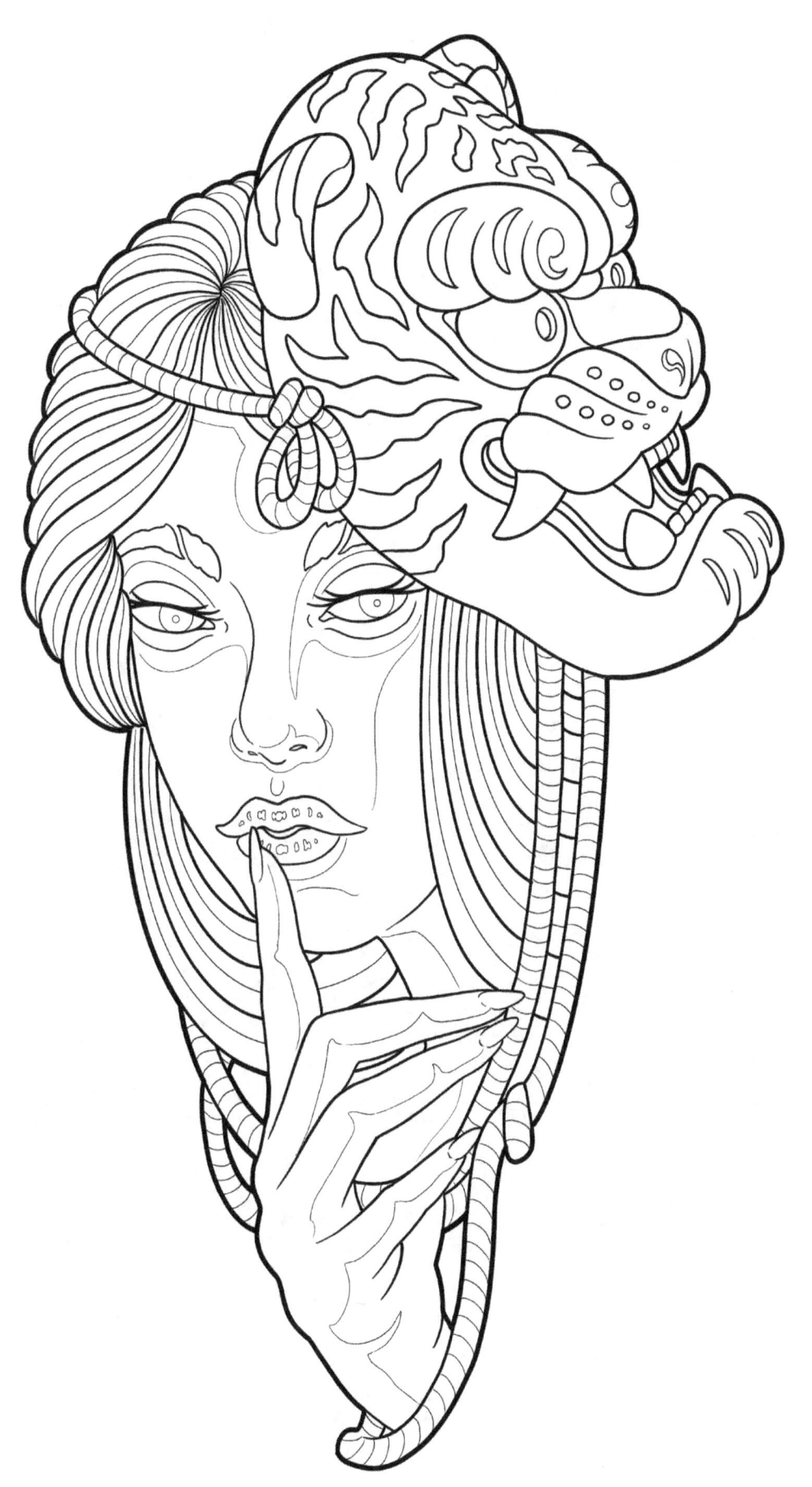

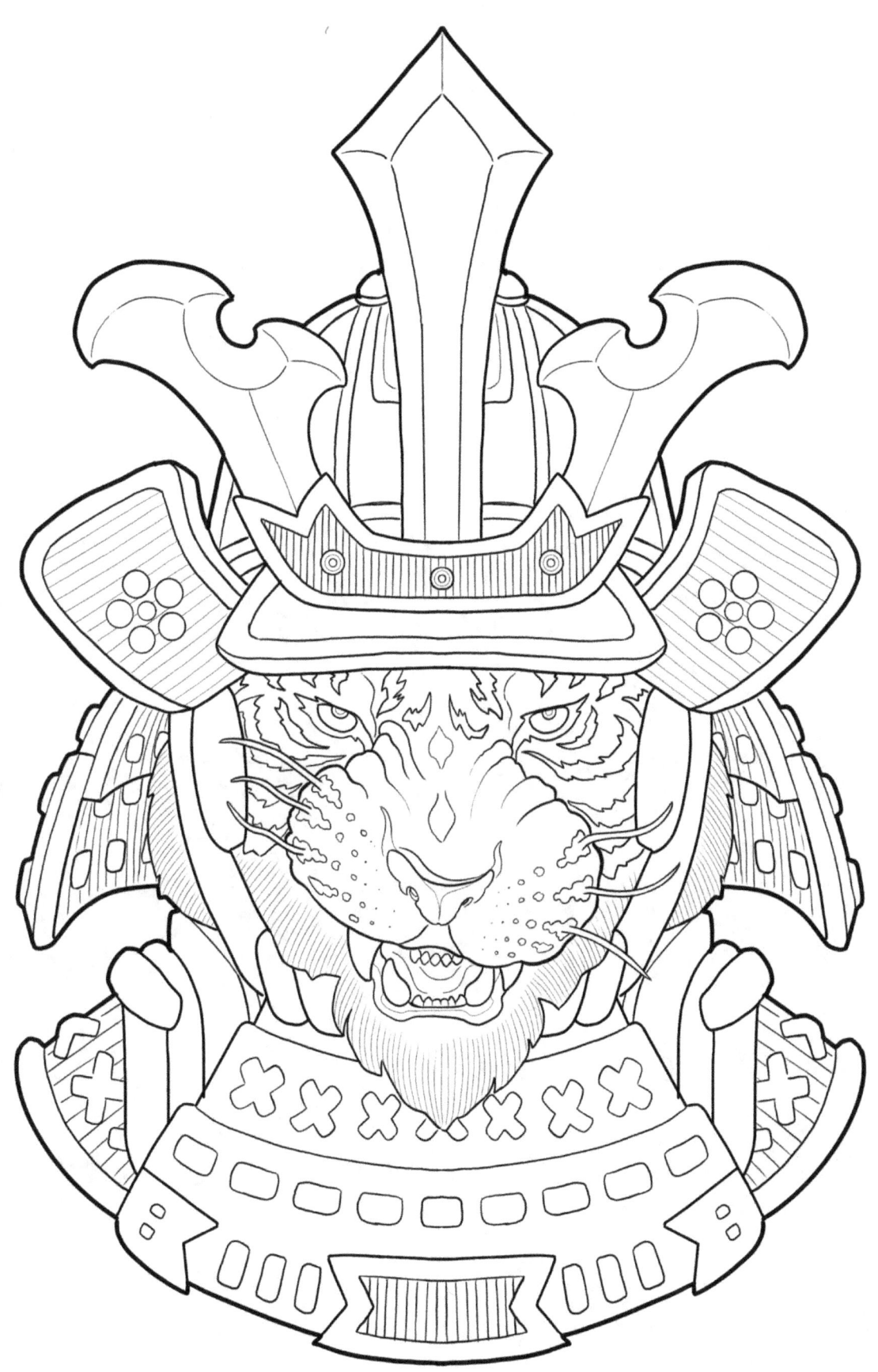

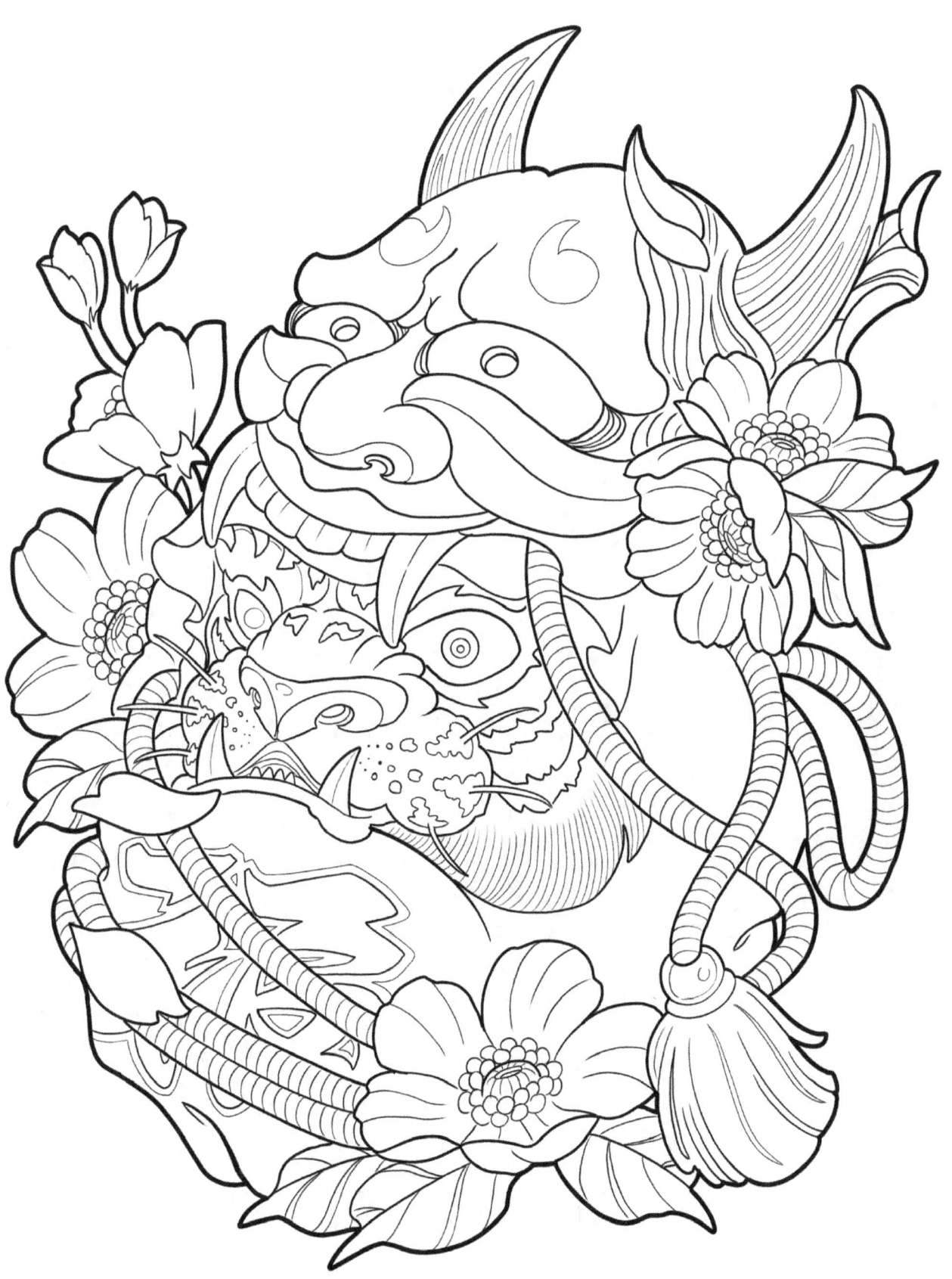

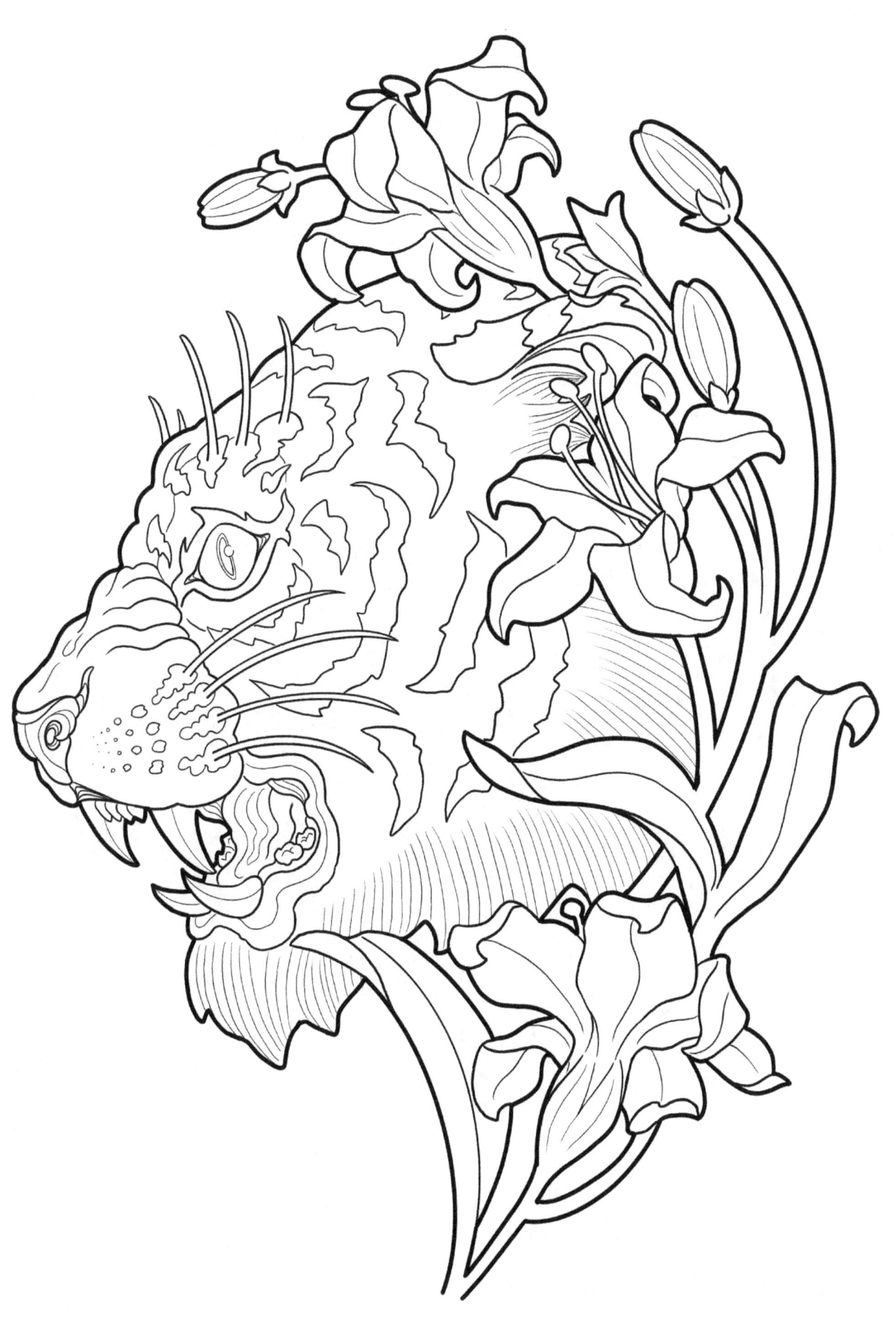

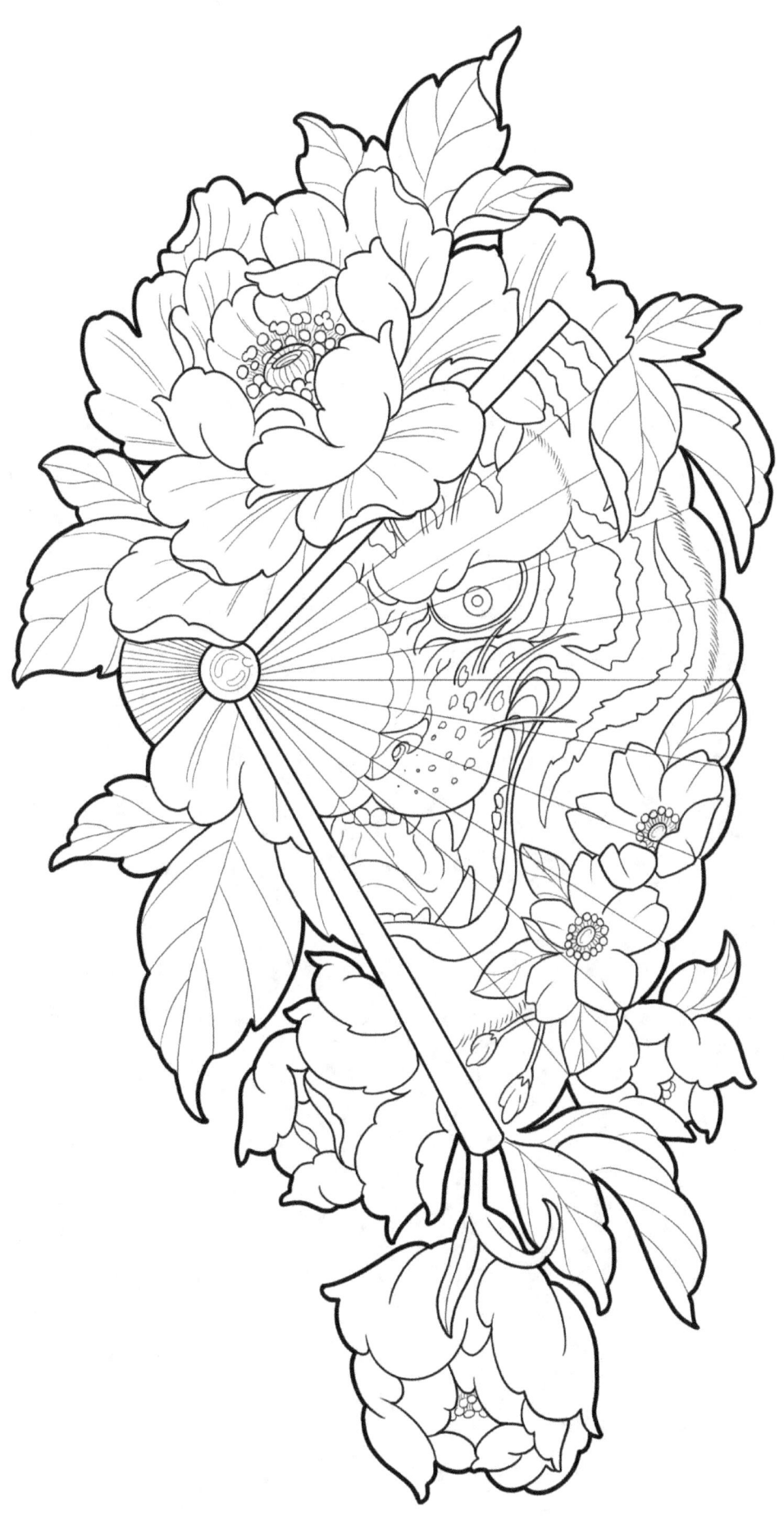

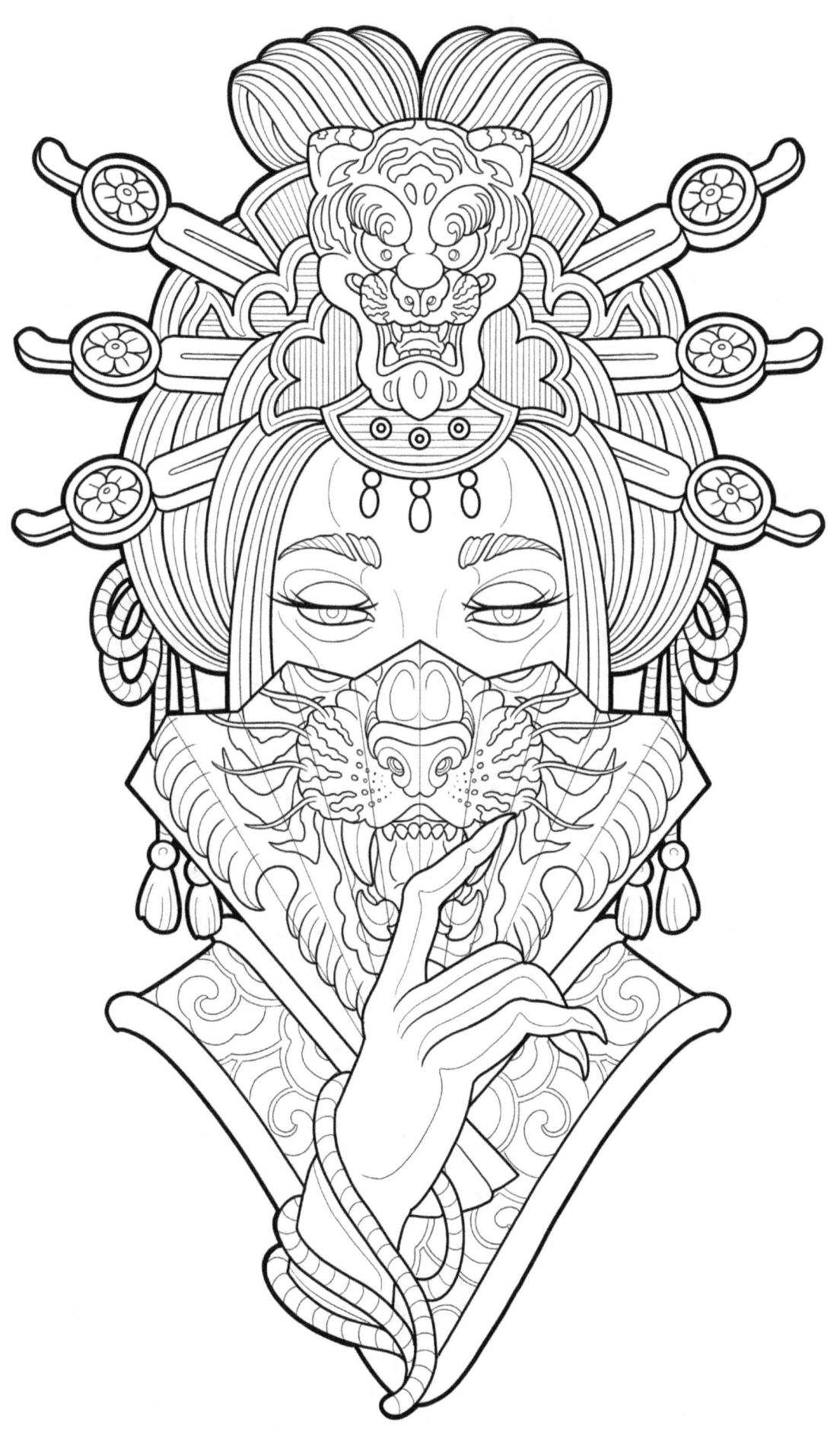

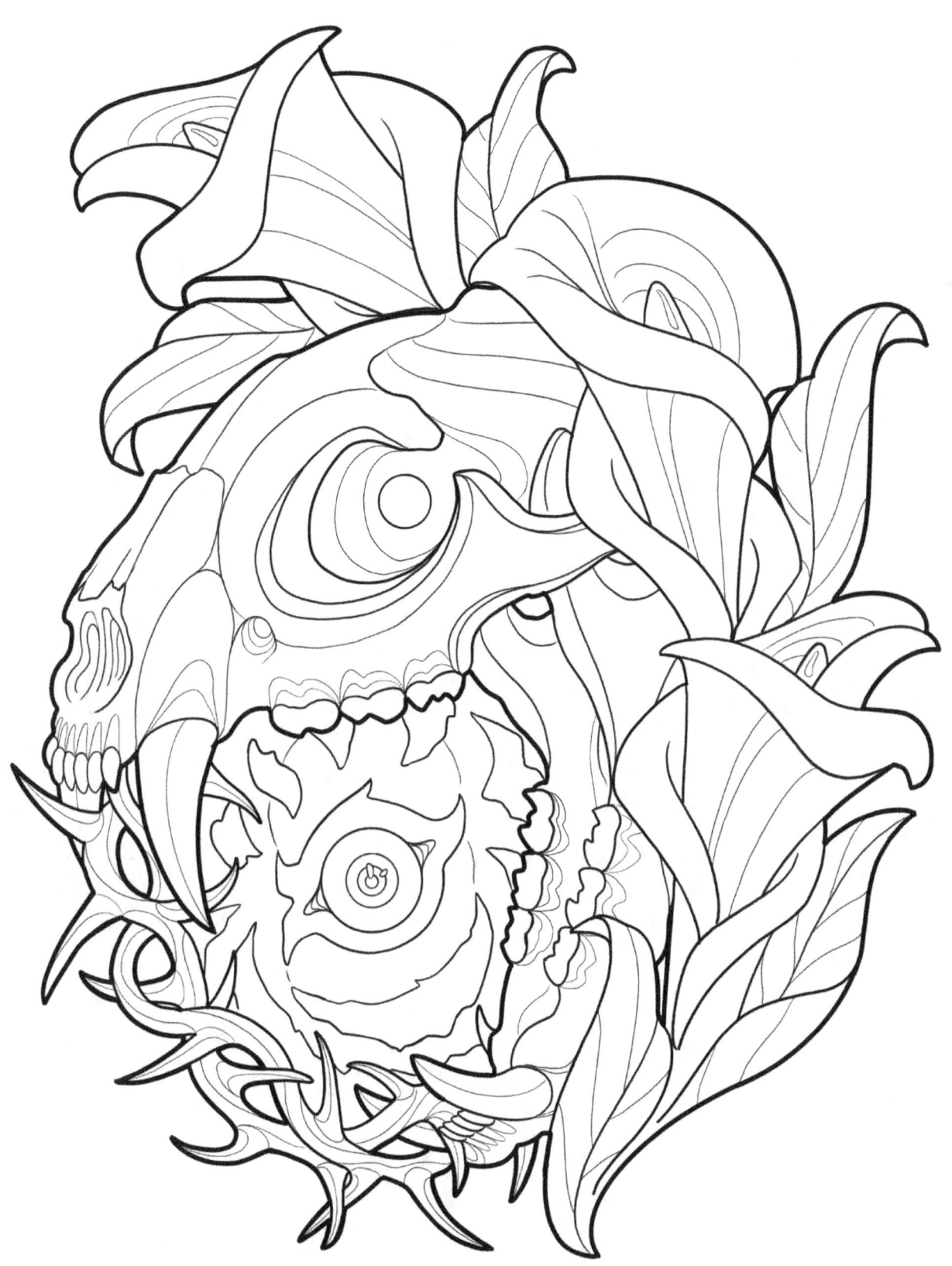

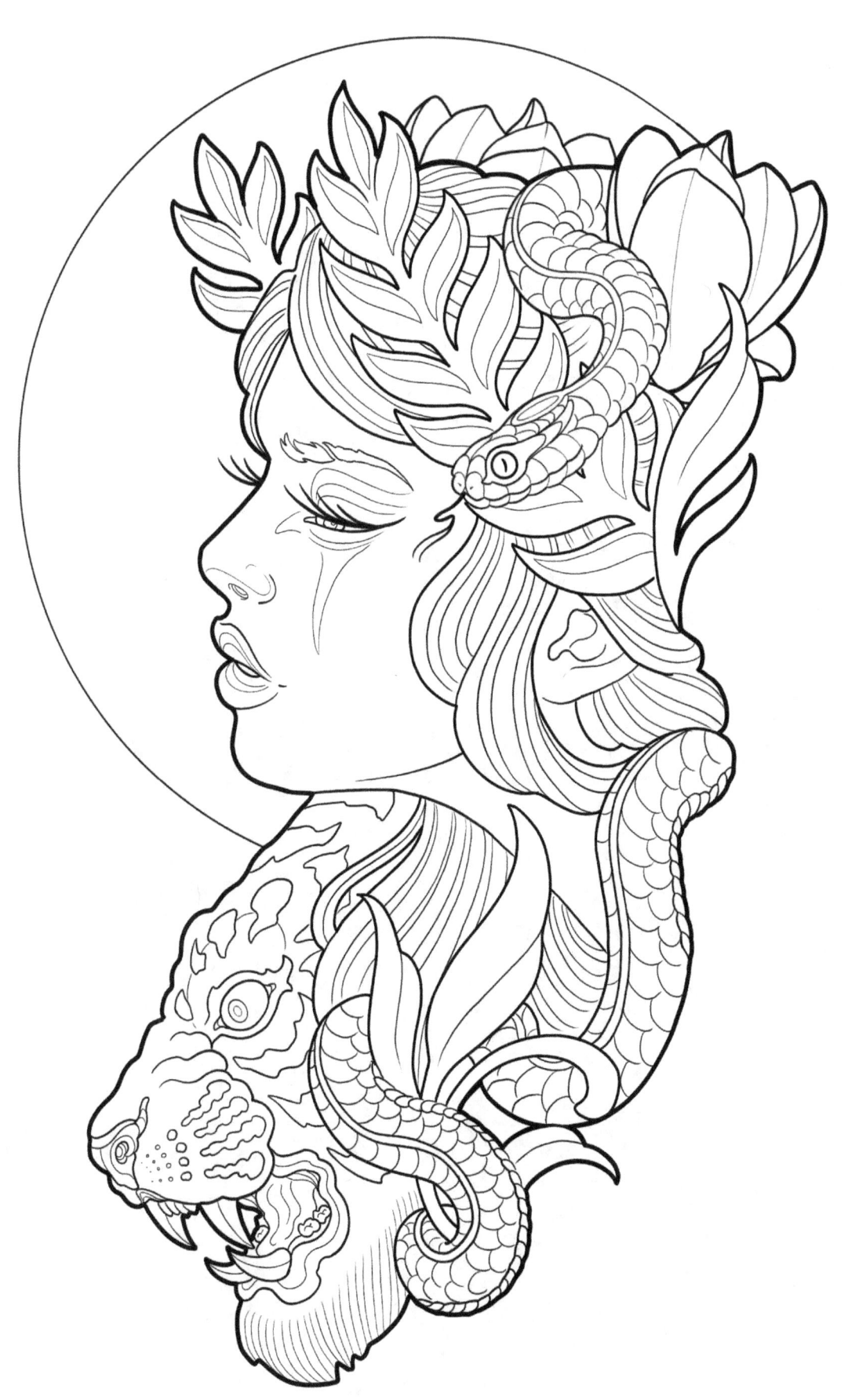

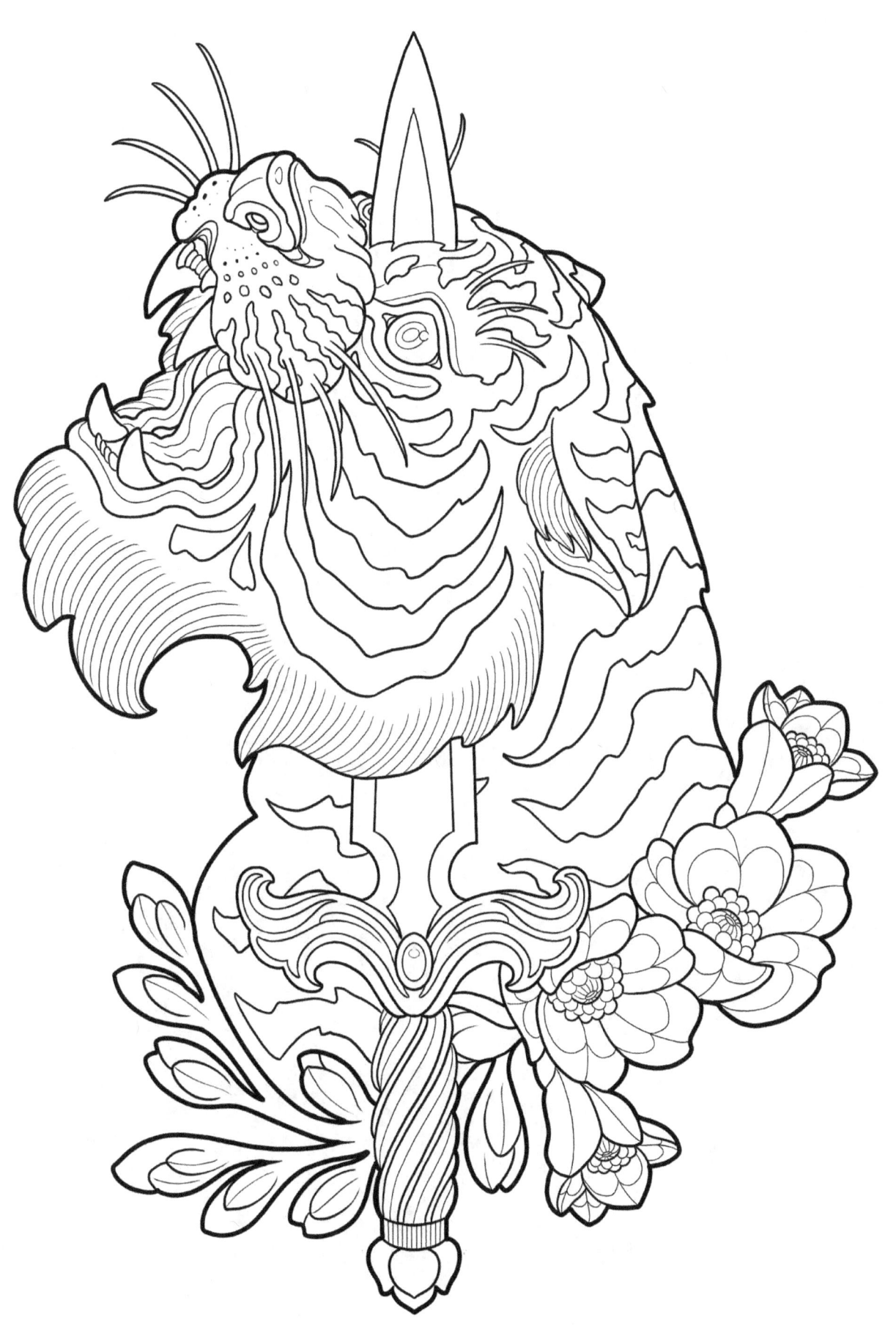

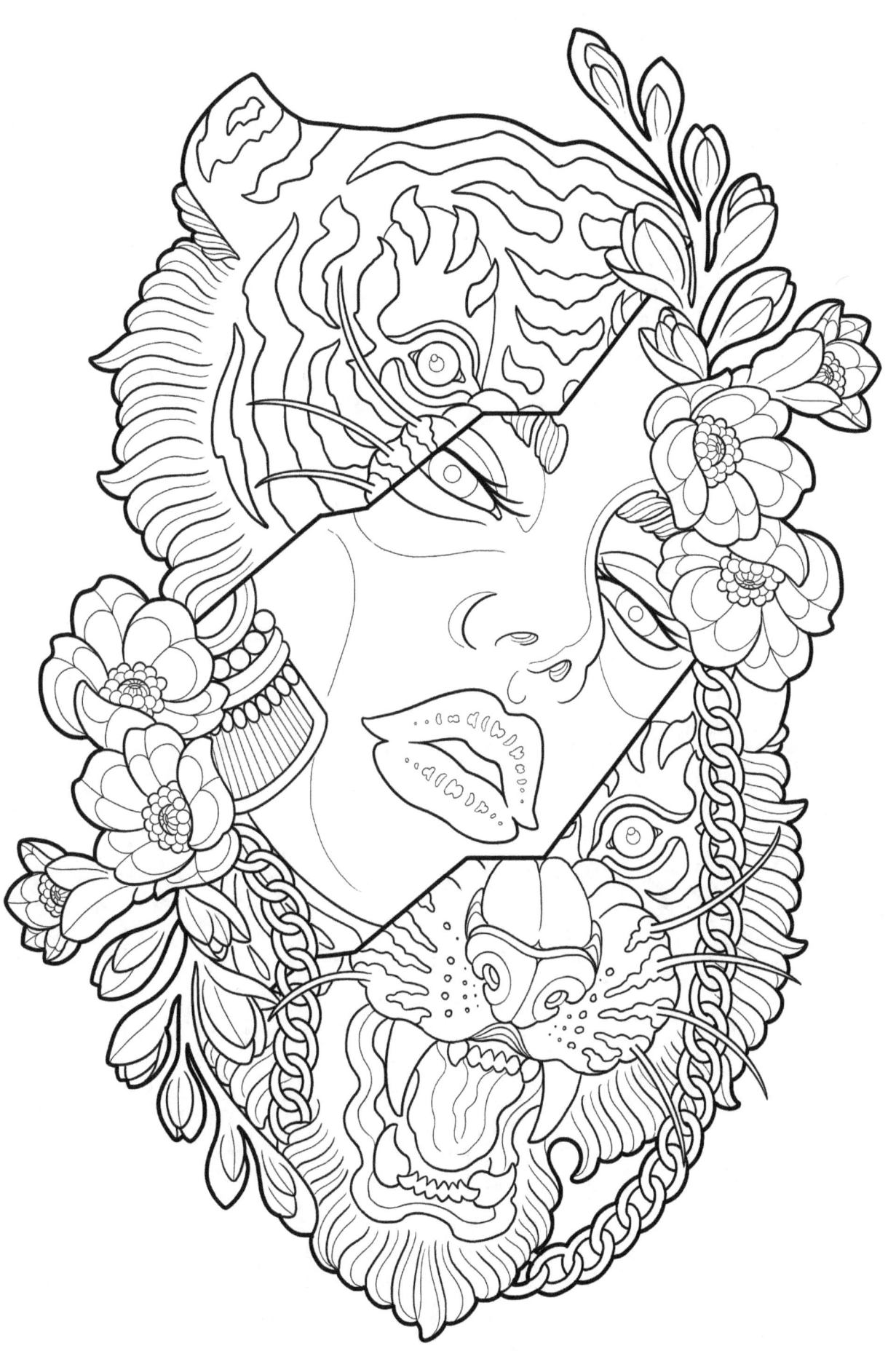

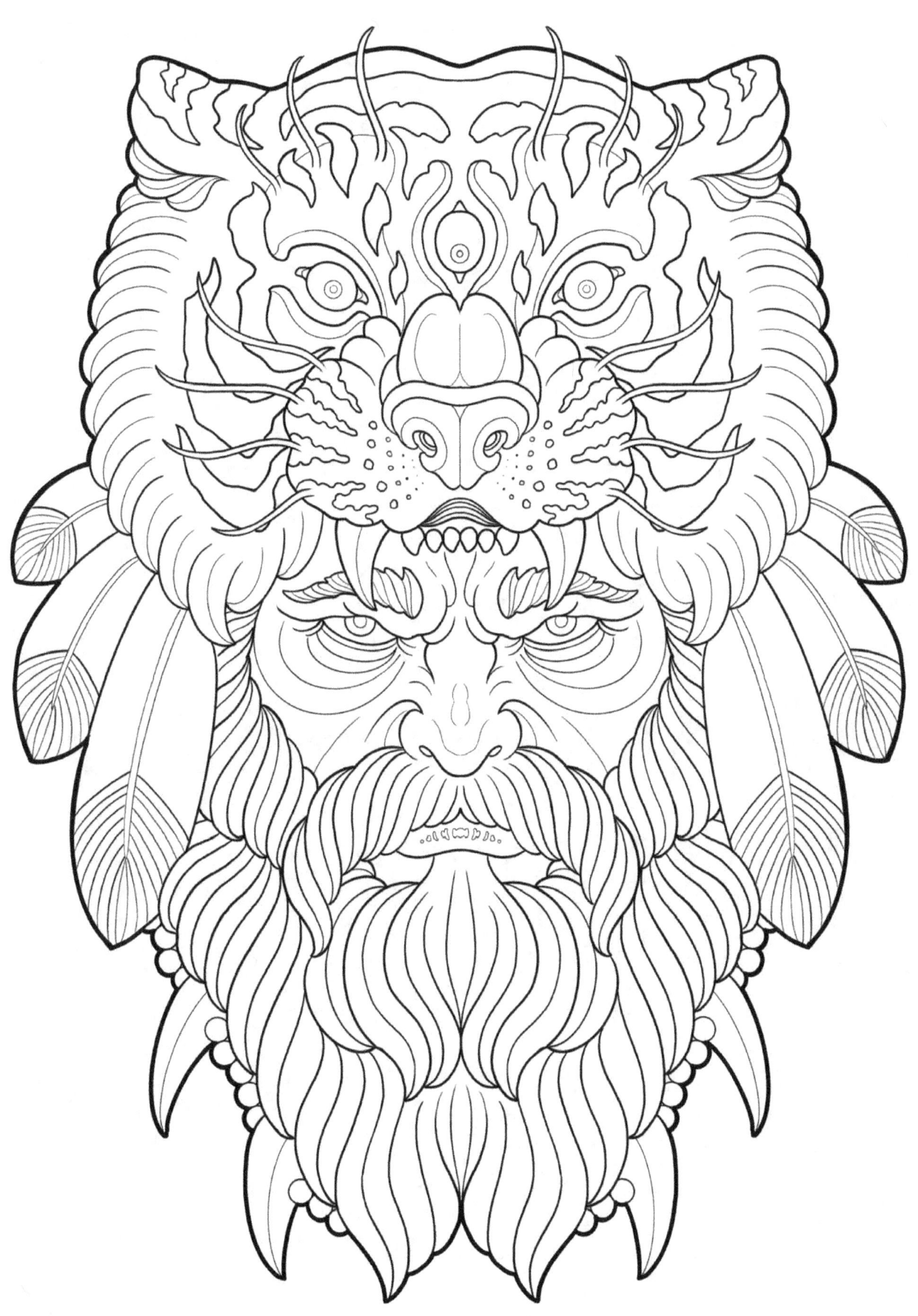

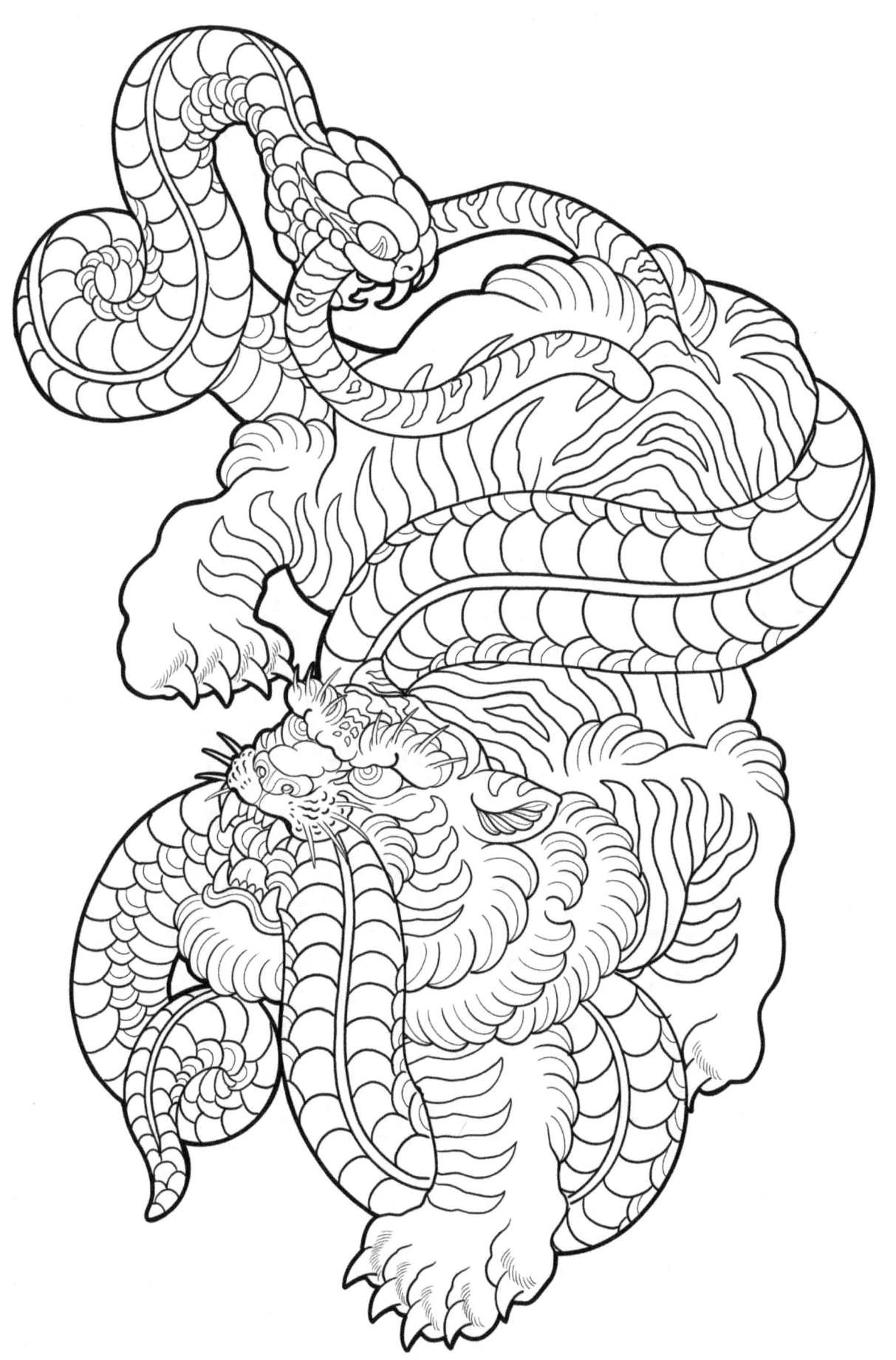

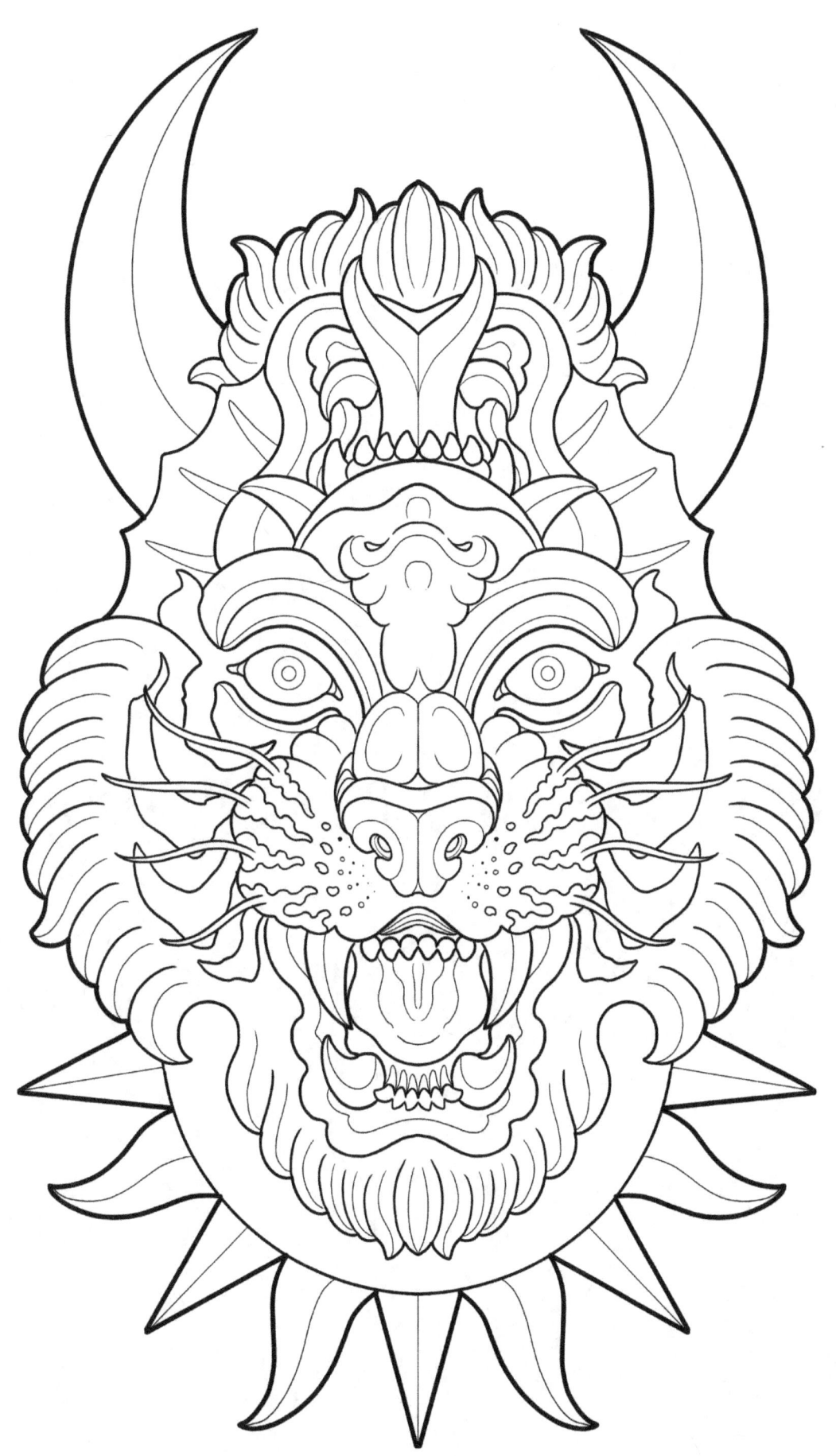

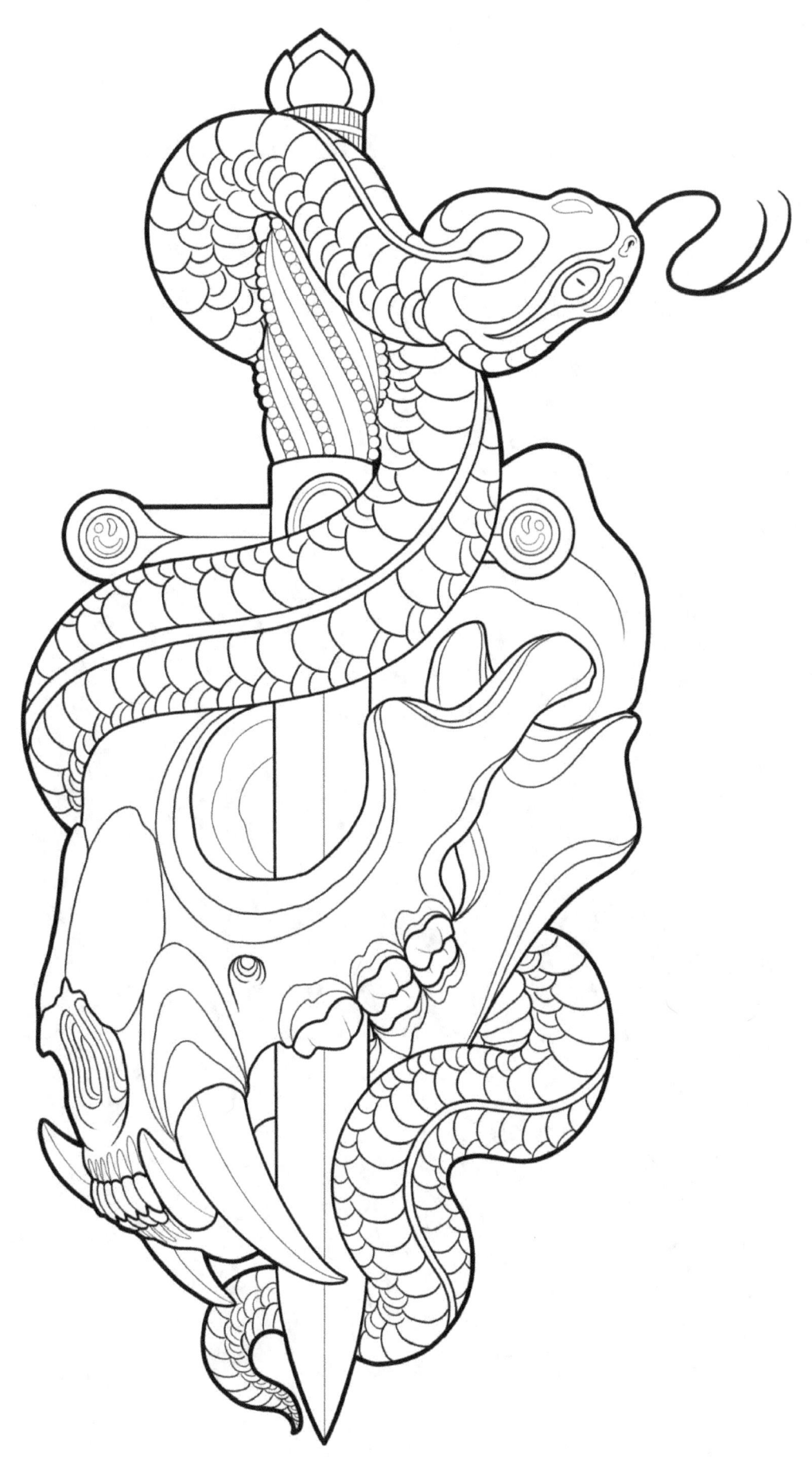

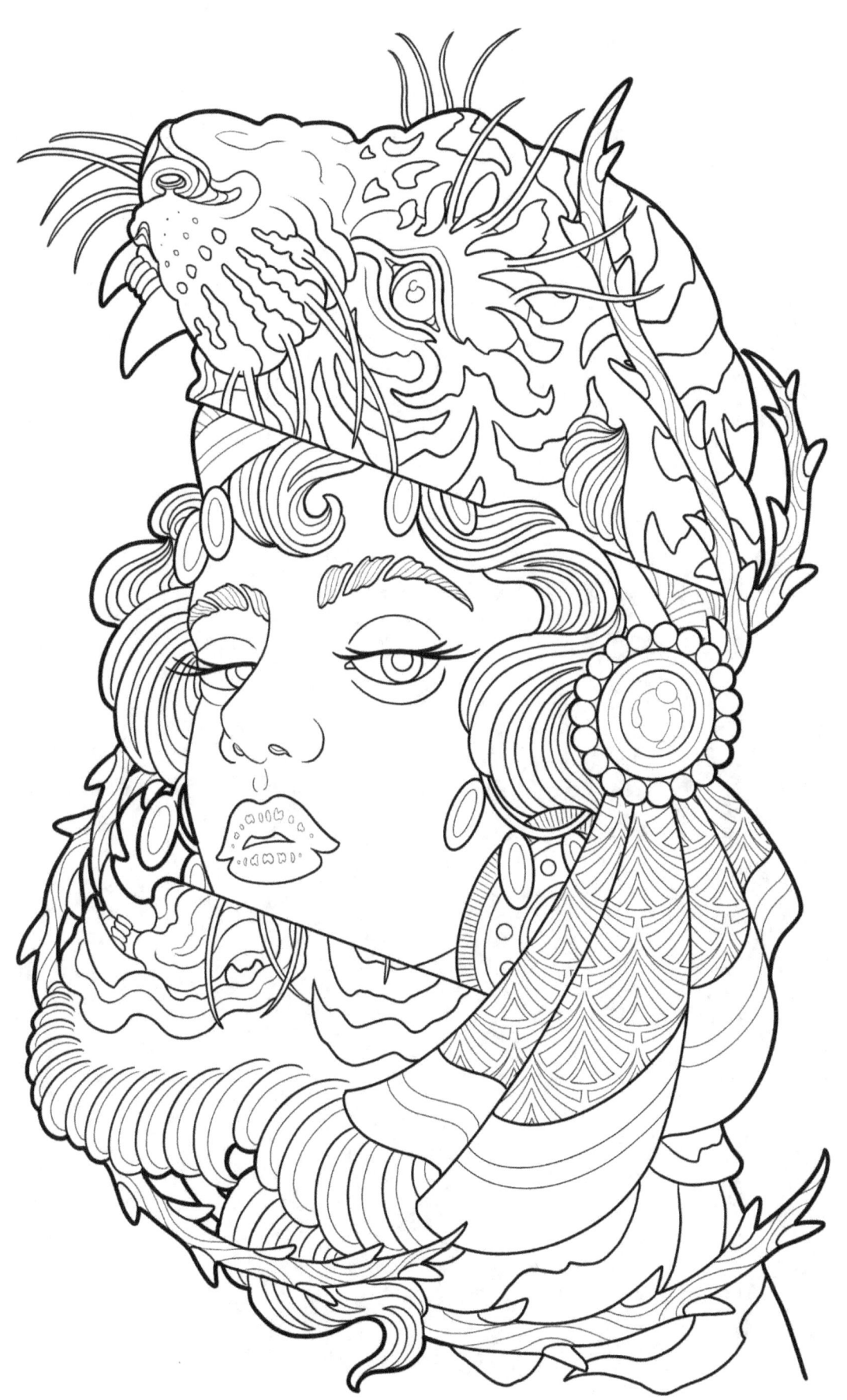

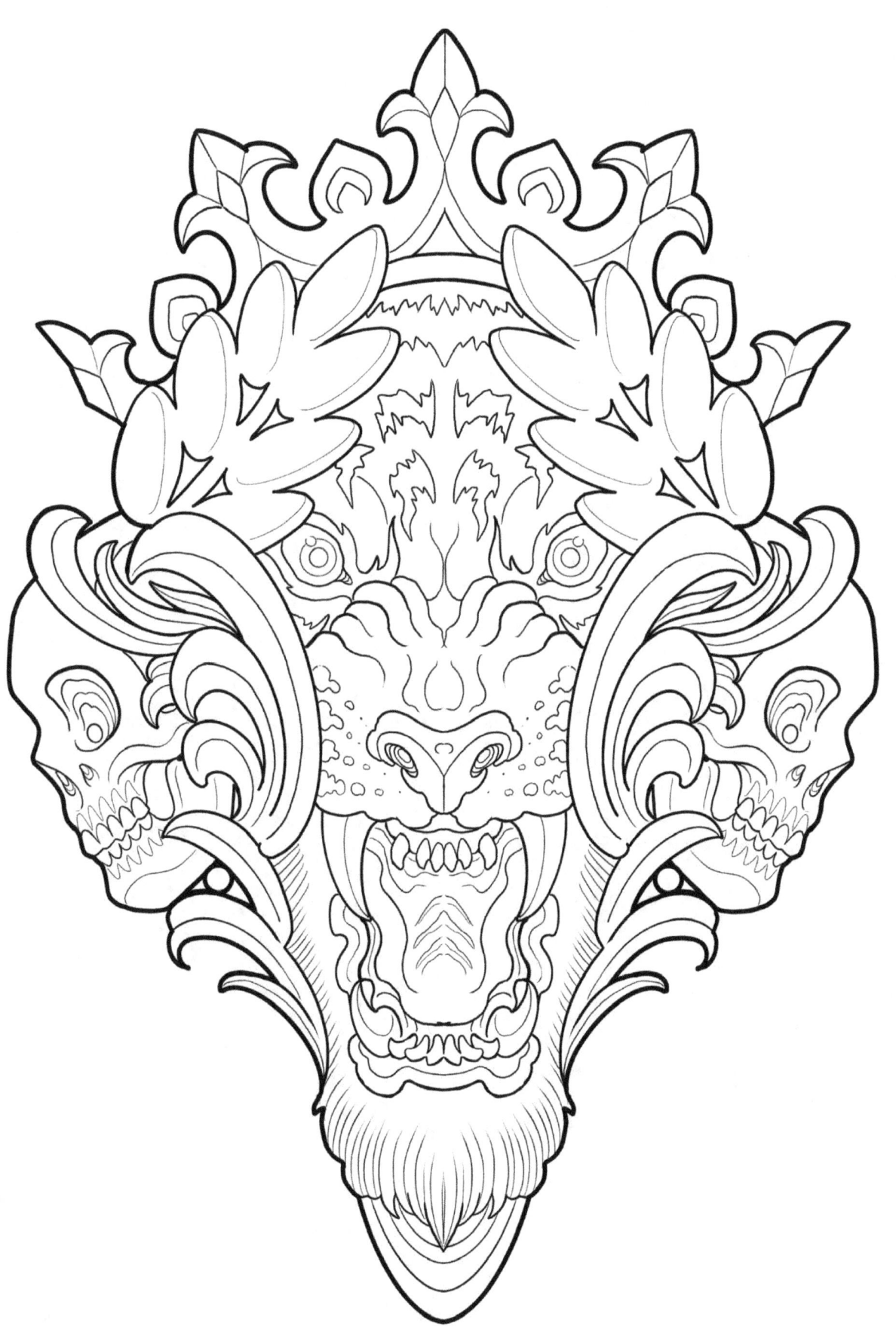

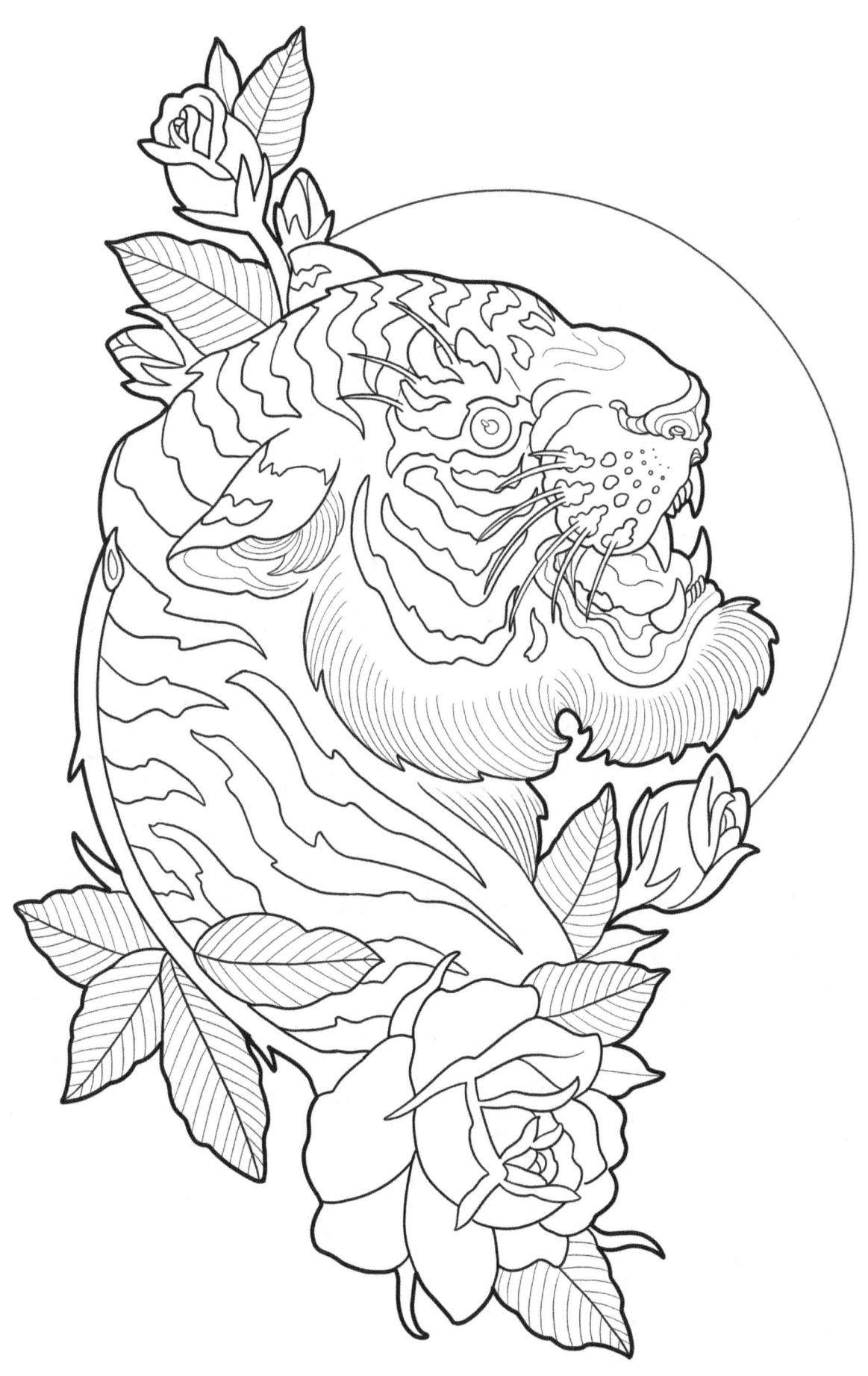

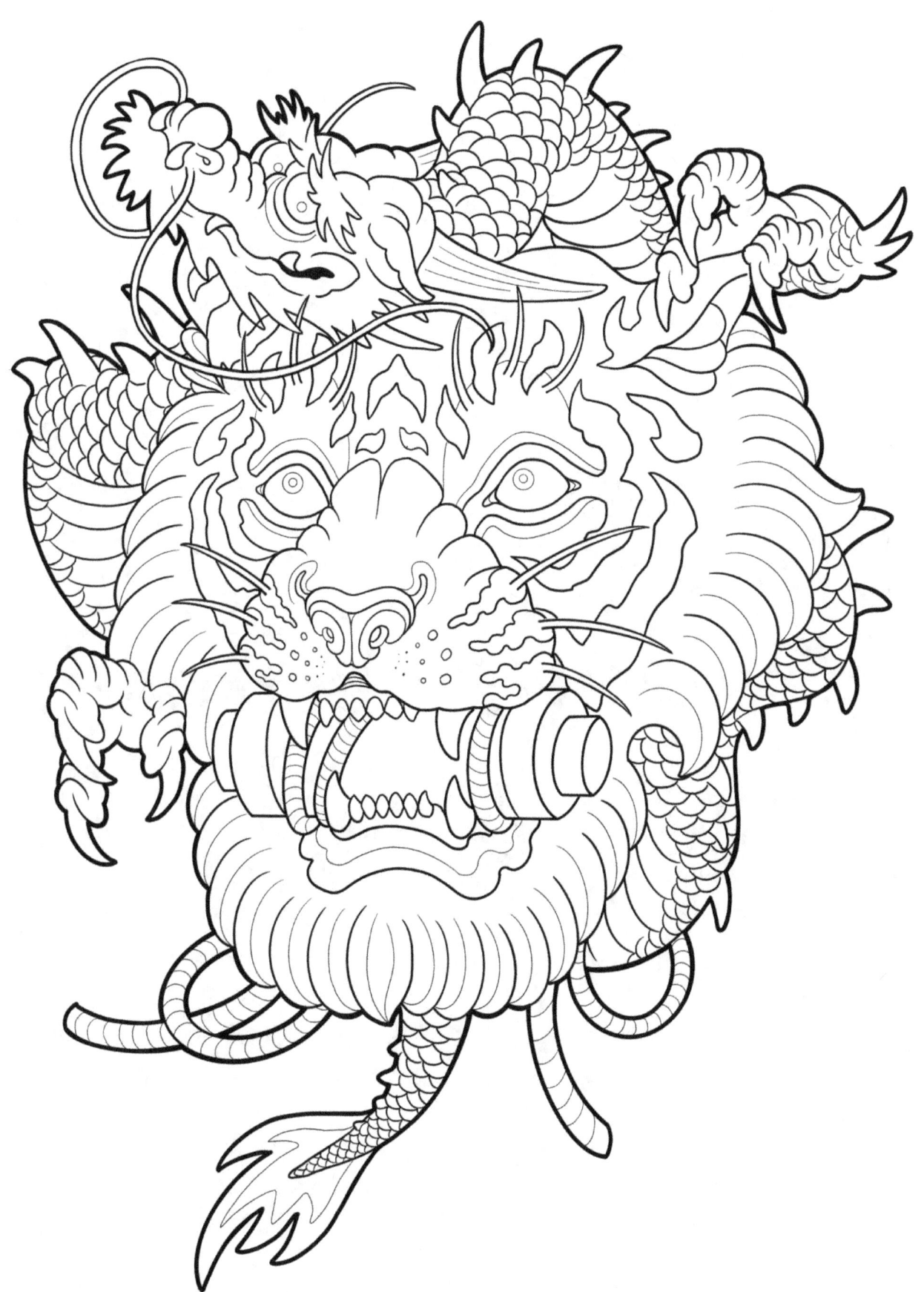

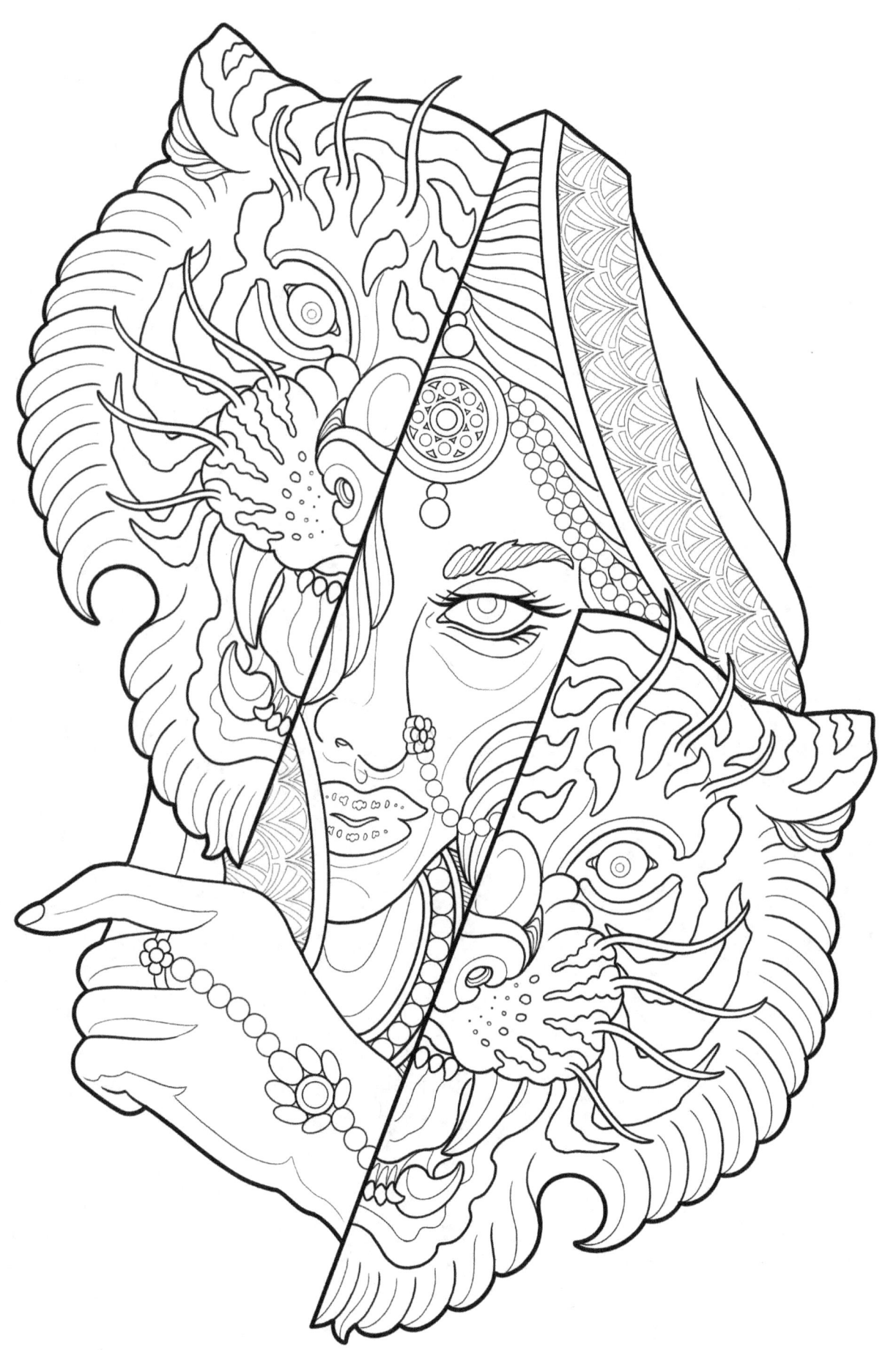

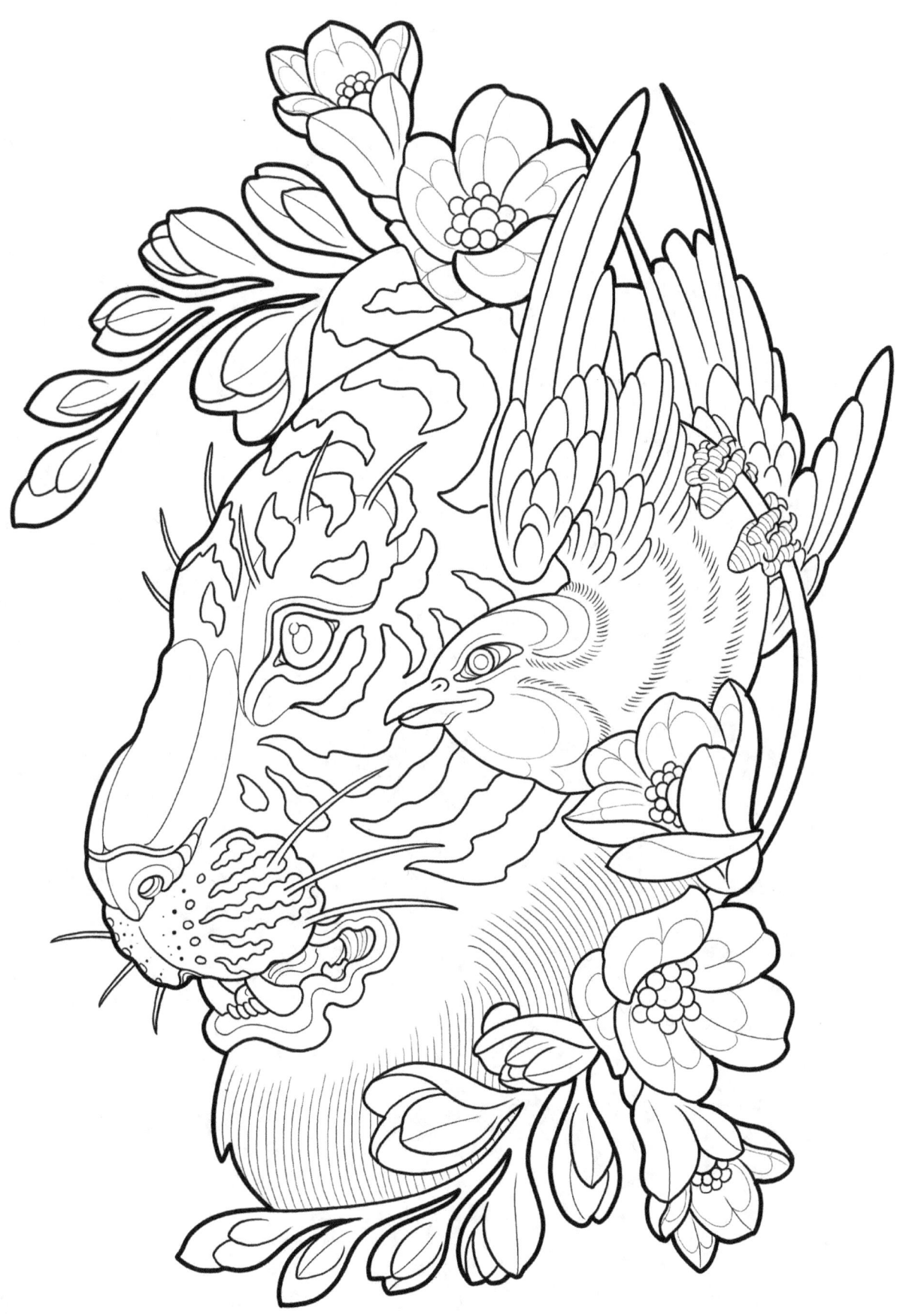

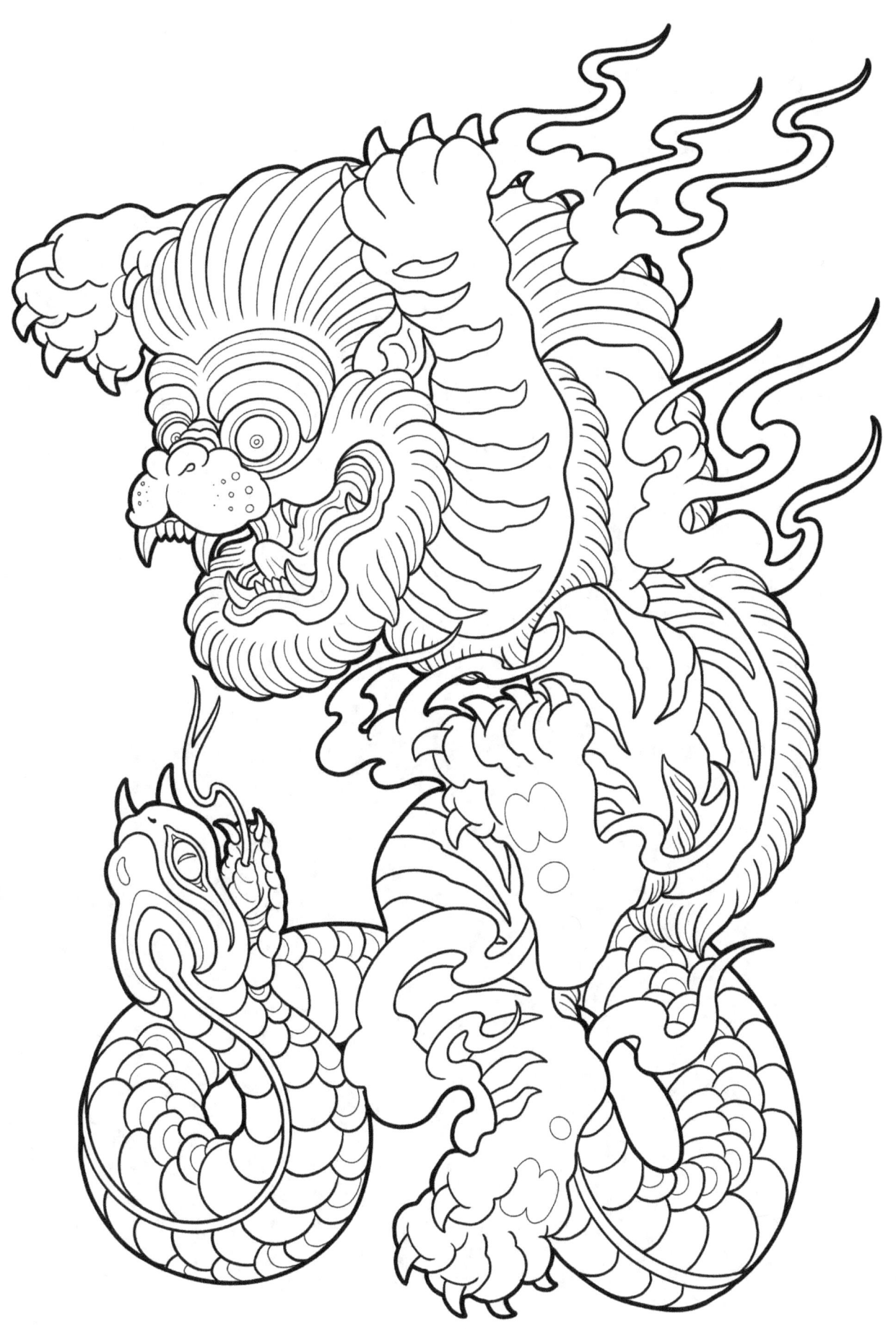

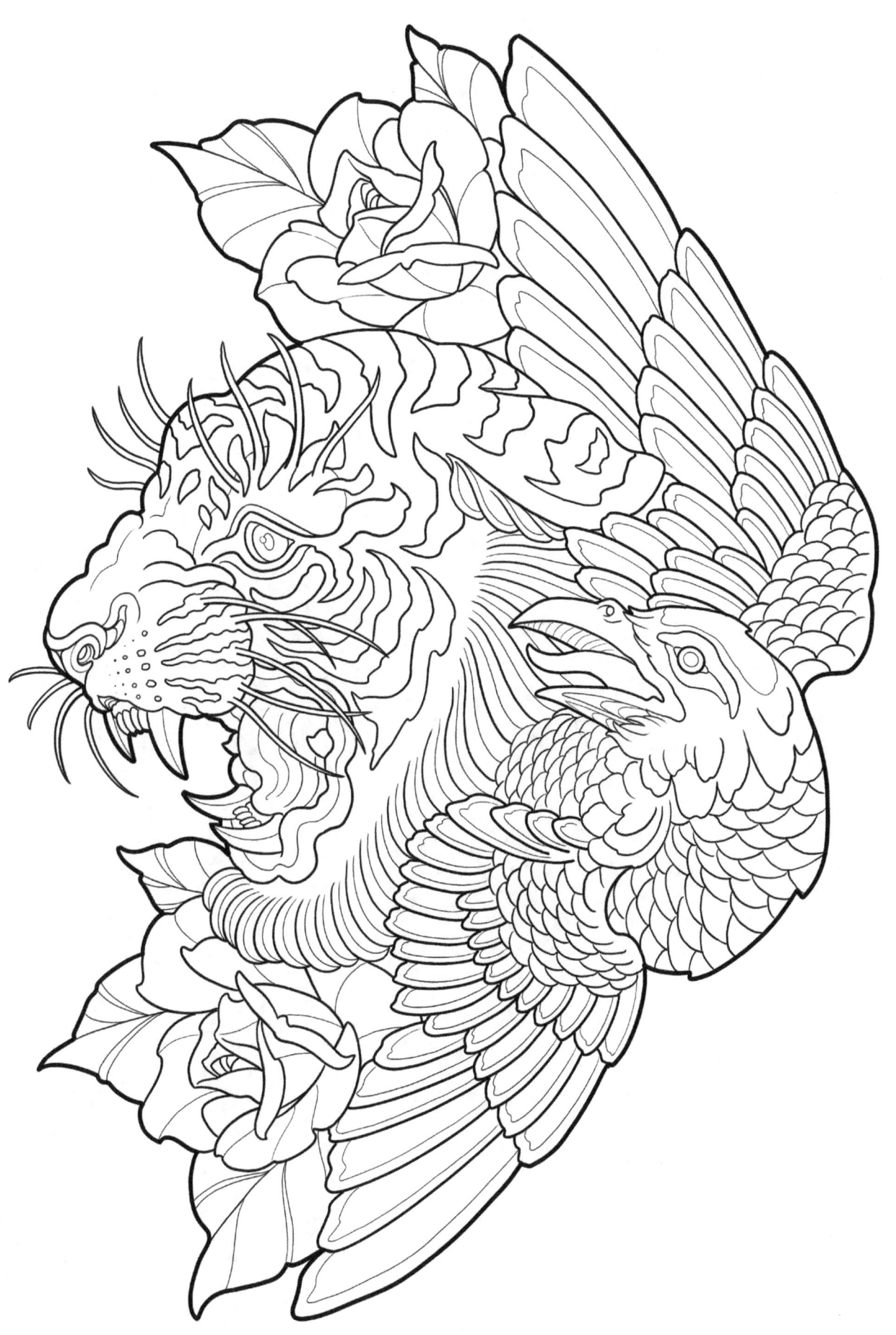

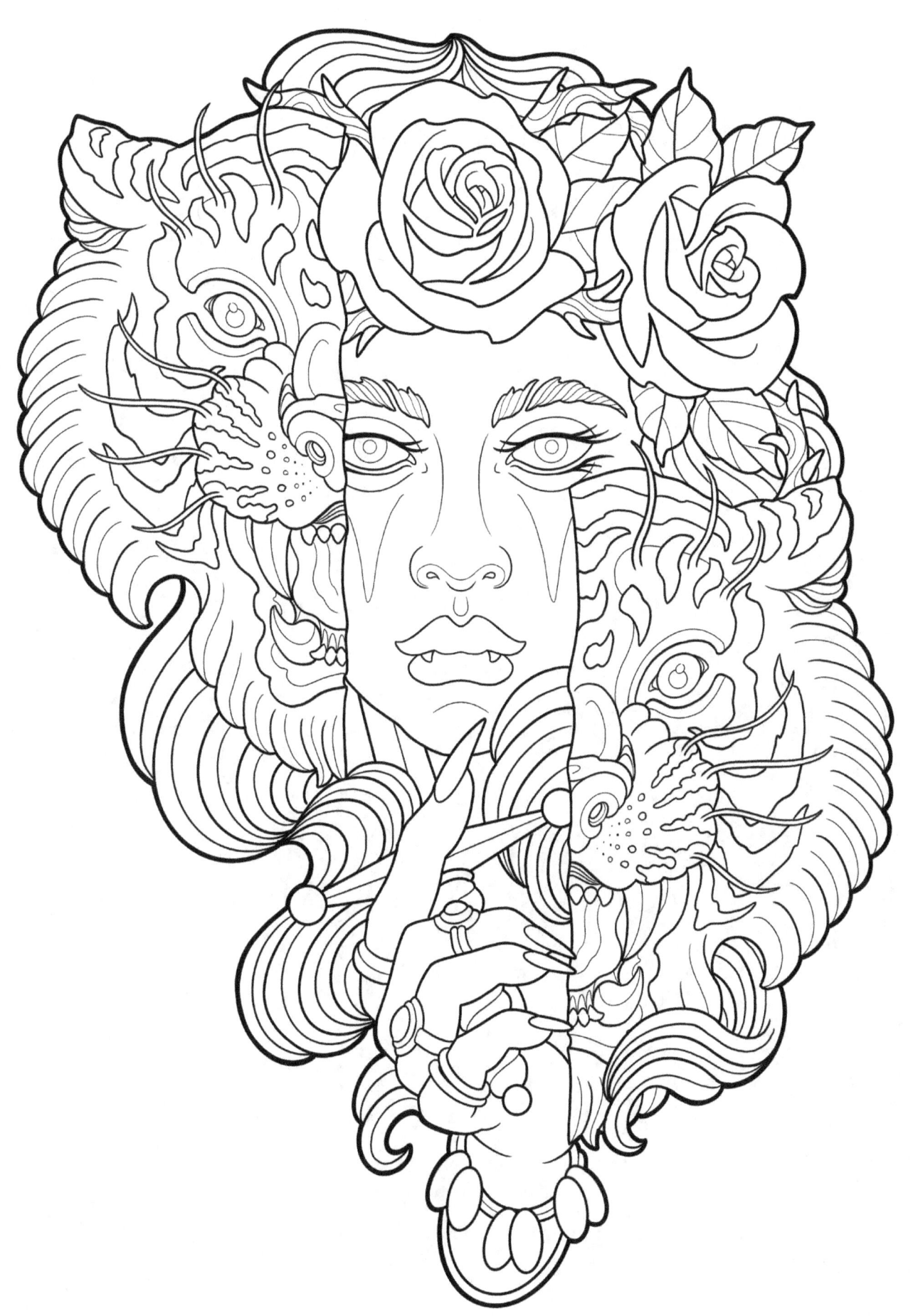

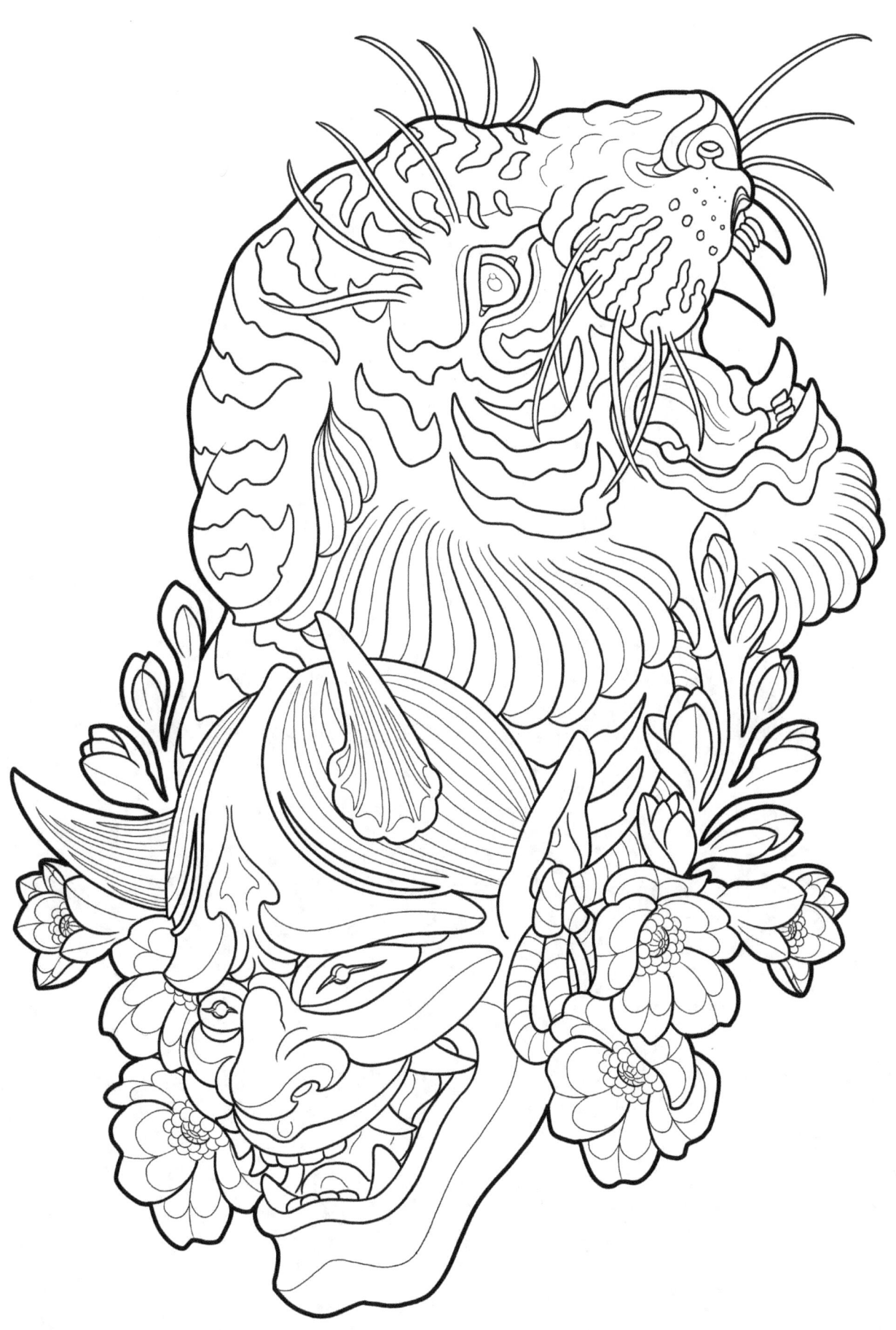

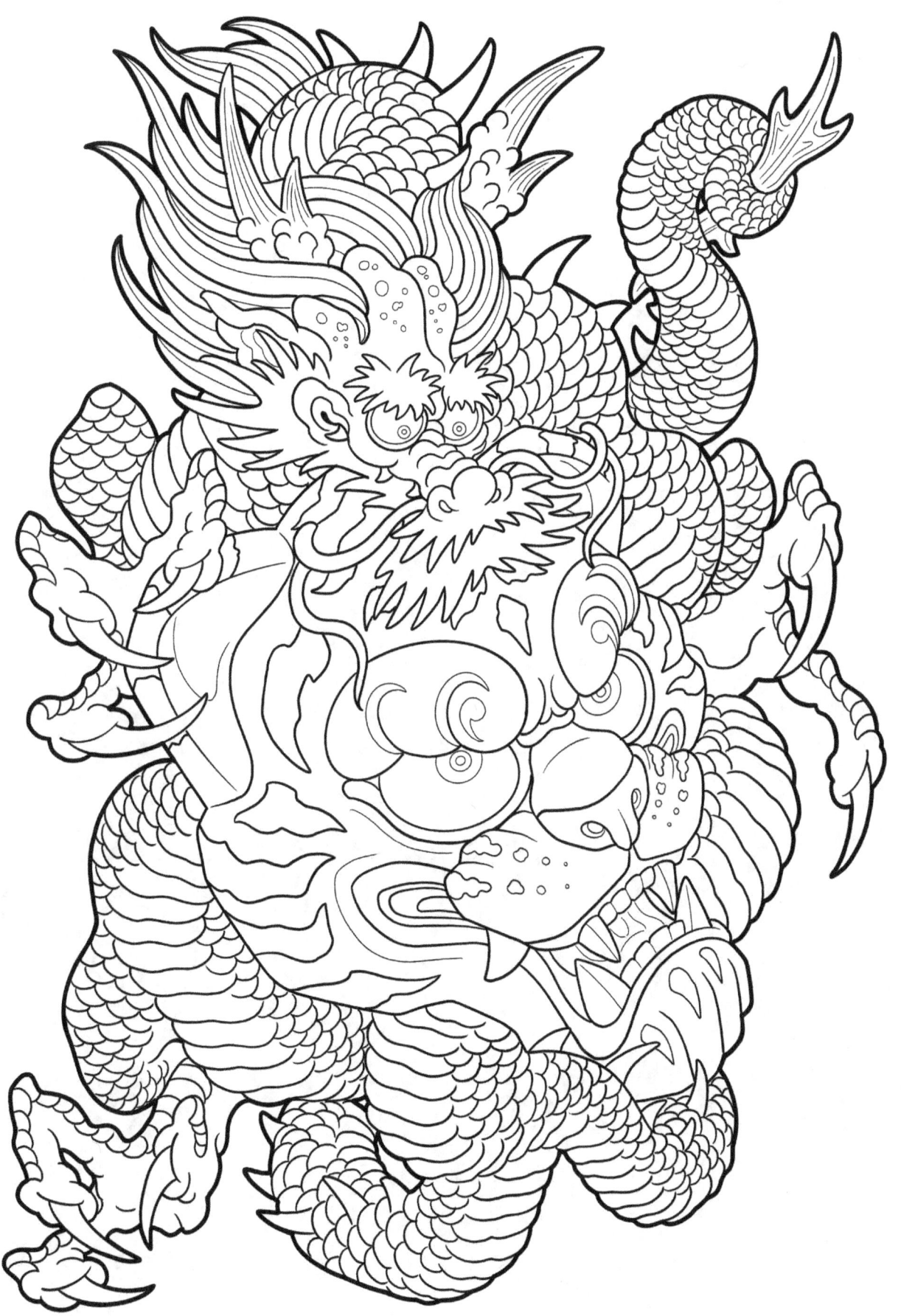

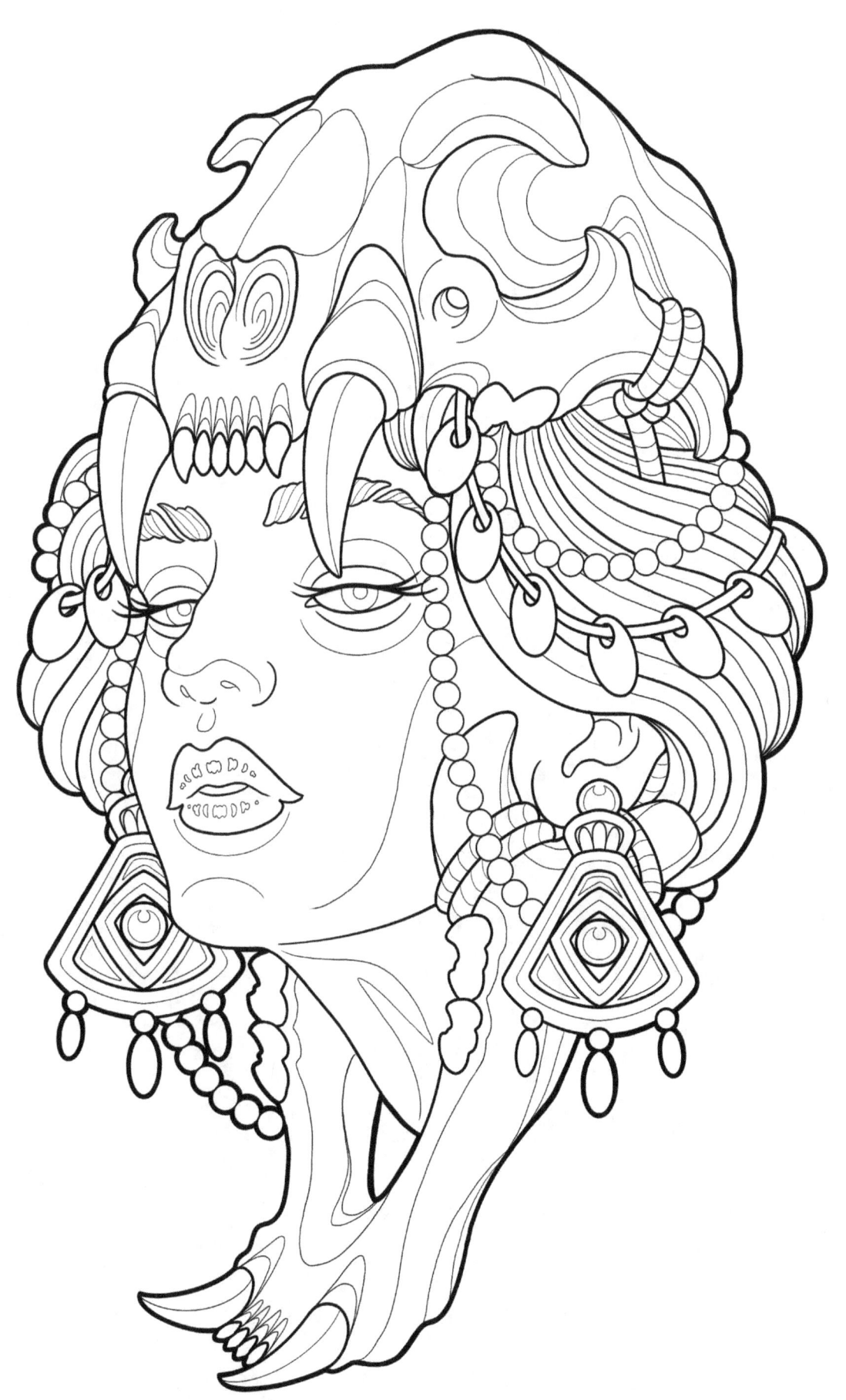

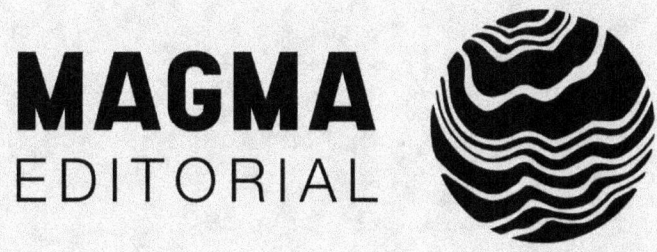

MAGMA
EDITORIAL

Thank you for purchasing **100 TIGERS TATTOO DESIGNS**.
We hope this book has exceeded your expectations.